To

Anne e & Christopher
With Kind Wishes
Henry

ANIMAL CRACKERS
IN COUNTRY PARKLAND

A.T.Bradford

by

Henry T. Bradford

Illustrations by Christine Sheppard

Grosvenor House
Publishing Limited

Henry T. Bradford is hereby identified as author of this
work in accordance with Section 77 of the Copyright, Designs
and Patents Act 1988

The book cover picture is copyright to Henry T. Bradford

This book is published by
Grosvenor House Publishing Ltd
28-30 High Street, Guildford, Surrey, GU1 3EL.
www.grosvenorhousepublishing.co.uk

A CIP record for this book
is available from the British Library

ISBN 978-1-78148-522-4

SYNOPSIS

This is a story of political corruption set in an animal woodland environment, it includes the premeditated murder of Wiggly Worm a pilot tunnel cutter employed by Digger Mole, and also of the slaughter of a colony of innocent spiders whom lived beneath the club house of a local privately owned golf club; and too of the retribution finally levied on the perpetrator of those crimes by spiders led by Black Widow spider, Managing Director of "Spiders International Limited", a company that specialised in international telecommunications with web sites in every corner of the earth.

The perpetrator of these political and murderous shenanigans was none other than Sly-Fox, (the former chairman of Reynards, Serpents, Stoats & Weasels; Civil Engineering Company Limited, a company more commonly known in the civil engineering business as RASCELS, which to the animals employed by it stood for "Robbers, Assassins, Scoundrels, Conniving Employer of Labouring Slaves" who, aided and abetted by Grass Snake, chief executive officer of Animal Country Parkland borough council, slyly persuaded his fellow elected colleagues on the council's Civil Engineering, Construction and Amenities Committee, into corruptly manipulating the awarding of all prime borough council civil engineering contracts, to his former employing company, Reynards, Serpents, Stoats & Weasels: Civil Engineering Company Limited.

However due to the murder of Wiggly Worm, a murder surreptitiously arranged to take place in the pilot tunnel Wiggly Worm was sent to excavate beneath a busy animal track; and worse still when it was later discovered at a coroners inquest, following Wiggly Worm's death, the soil through which the tunnel was being excavated was highly contaminated with toxic poisonous materials. A fact already known to Sly-Fox who was the site engineer in charge when the redundant gas works was demolished, the tunnel had to be abandoned. Sly-Fox and his associates were then obliged to called on Ms. Black Widow spider, of Spiders International Limited, a company that held all the patents under Royal Charter for the design and construction of bridges, to build a bridge over a dangerous Major Animal track, (M.A. track), as a safe access to and from a Junior High School for Young Animals.

That was when Sly-Fox over stepped the mark in fair-trading and business ethics, and when his troubles began in earnest, and which led finally to his downfall by trial at the hands of "Spiders International Limited".

CONTENTS

THE LIST OF ILLUSTRATIONS

By

Christine Sheppard.

PROLOGUE

The Black Widow spider's secretary, Funnel Web spider, tapped gently on her Managing Directors office door and was ordered: 'Come! What is it now? You know I'm busy.'

'Yes, but I thought you would like to know the news has just come through on our international web site receiver. Sly-Fox has publicly announced he is about to retire from Reynards & Serpents Civil Engineering and Construction Company Limited, or as that company is more commonly know throughout the civil engineering world, RASCELS'.

The Black Widow put down her pen, looked up at her secretary with her eyes half closed, then began tapping four of her eight feet, and blinking her eight eyes before saying in utter surprise: 'Oh! Really!'

'Yes, and the message on the web was he is retiring to a place in England, a small county town by the name of Animal Country Parkland.

'Oh! What do you think he's up to? I bet he's up to some sort of evil shenanigans. He always is that crafty devil. So what else did the message have to report, besides Sly-Fox's intended retirement?'

'Only the usual sort of guff the news media puts about, such as Sly-Fox being able to settle down to enjoy a well earned rest and a quiet life in the country; and of his hoping to be able to give to the community of Animal Country Parkland assistance in developing community facilities by possibly putting himself forward for election onto the borough council where, he said, his world wide experience in civil engineering and construction may be of some value to that county borough.'

'Yes! Well that crafty blackguard would say that, wouldn't he? But if you look up his antecedents on our web network records, I'm sure you will find, if my memory serves me correctly, RASCELS had civil engineering contracts in Animal Country Parkland some years ago. It was a redundant gas works, which had been illegally built on common land a century before. RASCELS acquired the site together with a large plot of land under squatters rights law. You had better send out a message over our International Web Transmission System to all spiders that live in and around Animal Country Parkland, and order them report to me on anything untoward Sly-Fox gets up to. I'll leave the wording of the message to you, OK.'

'Yes,' replied Funnel Web Spider. 'I'll get on to that right away.' She then went quickly but quietly out of Ms. Black Widow Spider's office, to send messages off immediately to all the spiders that lived in the sleepy, quiet, and peaceful township of Animal Country Parkland. The message read:

"Beware. Sly-Fox is on his way to live among you in Animal Country Parkland. He is not only a Sly-Fox by name; he is even slyer by nature. He is devious as well as being cunning, and there is little doubt he has ambitious intentions he intends to carry out in his new habitat. Be assured he will stop at NOTHING to achieve his objective; I repeat, NOTHING. Be on your guard."

By my order, Black-Widow Spider, Managing Director, "Spiders International Limited."

However, unbeknown to Funnel-Web spider, her boss sat in her office mulling over the message she had just received regarding Sly-Fox. "What is he up to?" she mumbled to herself. "Why should he want to retire to Animal Country Parkland?" Then she remembered as a thought struck her – the old gasworks – it has to do with the old gasworks site. I'll just have to be patient and wait to see how the situation develops, when that conniving manipulator in fox-fur begins his usual underhand corruptive antics in Animal Country Parkland. So I shall, by Golly. So I shall.

Part 1

Animal Crackers in
Animal Country Parkland

The fading light of the full moon began to cast long shadows over the countryside as it was setting in the distant horizon, its long night's work over. It was as though the moon's waning light was fearful of meeting the bright rays of the new day's sun; a bright ball of fire; a phoenix in outer space; a blazing orbiting star that dies at night and is resurrected each dawn; a luminous

globe whose rays steadily began to reflect its light beneath a canopy of cumulus clouds, clouds that were drifting across the early morning sky, white clouds that to the mind's eye appeared as though they were emulating a flight of swans, flying over a lake of crystal clear blue water. It was such a peaceful, idyllic scene, until...

A flash of forked lightning, like a finger of doom, zigzagged its way across the heavens followed by a crash of thunder that echoed back and forth between the surrounding hills. Then a cockerel crowed, awakened by the dawn breaking. Almost in unison, others of its ilk followed with their clarion calls reverberating throughout the countryside. *Cock-a-doodle-doo, Cock-a-doodle-doo,* was to be heard far and wide, echoing throughout the animal kingdom. These were the signals for large eyed barn owls, blind bats too, to take the crowing of the cockerels as their cue to abandon their night of hunting, as did all those other nocturnal animals that prowl about the woodlands from dusk till dawn, each one of them quickly making its separate way, as fast as it could, back to the safety of its own nest, roost, den, lair or burrow. All of them that is, except for those large herbivorous animals, quadrupeds that graze on herbage in the open fields by day and night; cows, horses, pigs and sheep. Those large domesticated animals with nothing to fear from the small, indigenous, carnivorous predators of the open countryside and woodlands, that had been out all night hunting for prey. On the other hand, the daylight active animals began to rise from their slumbers, rudely awakened by the raucous cockerels' clarions and the twittering of the morning birds' chorus. In woodland glades, underground burrows and farmyards, young animal's mothers were busily preparing breakfast for their offspring before setting off with them to school.

Animal Country Parkland Borough Council had built a 'Primary High School for Young Animals' beside a busy Major Animal Track, (M A track), on scrubland that had been 'free gifted' to it by Reynard's, Serpents, Stoats and Weasels Civil Engineering and Construction Company Limited, more commonly known within the civil engineering industry as RASCELS. It was land that had been known by the Chairman of Reynard's and Serpents, Sly-Fox, but not by the local inhabitants of the woodlands and countryside at that time, to be classified as 'unfit for agricultural or development purposes' because the site had some years previously been the site of Animal Country Parkland Borough Council's gasworks.

The redundant gasworks site was known to the borough council's Planning and Development Department to be heavily contaminated with noxious deposits of arsenic and heavy metals – by-products of the process of extracting gas from coal.

(The method of producing coal gas, [an operation that had been carried out on the site for many years], was by baking coal to *900-centigrade* [*1,650-fahrenhelt*] in closed retorts. The volatile heated coal gas was floated off and its heat reduced by a system of cooling pipes. After which its coke, [a residue from the coal], had then been carried by pack ponies to a steelworks, to be used as fuel in its blast furnaces. After its extraction from coal, the gas was piped into nearby gasometers till required for use).

The consequence of this *gas extraction process* had been that coal was turned into coke, coal tar and many other by-products; materials that had been extracted during this process by condensation, after which other valuable materials such as dyes, had been removed by dissolving them in water. It was a process that could also be used to extract oil from coal.

The 'local wreck', as the gasworks site was better known by the inhabitants of Animal Country Parkland, after its abandonment by its previous owners when natural gas was discovered in the North Sea, (that was before it became a school site), had previously been common land held for the use of all free animals in the countryside. That was many centuries before it had been *snatched* from their forebears under Land Enclosure Laws passed in the House of Common Animals and then sold by the new landowner to be developed as a gasworks site during the Reign of Queen Victoria (1837-1901).

However, it had been long before that event, in fact, when Elizabeth 1 (1533-1603) was Queen of England and King Oberon and Queen Titania sat on the Fairies Throne, after a performance of William Shakespeare's *A Midsummer Night's Dream* performed in the library at Windsor Castle, King Oberon had decreed,

"The woodland known as Animal Country Parkland shall be left open as common land for the use and benefit of all the common animals of the countryside, in perpetuity." It was, however, a gesture that was to be stolen from them under 18th and 19th century Land Enclosure Laws, put in place by corruptly elected politicians in what were later to become known as 'the Rotten Boroughs', that is county boroughs, in which only aristocrats and the landed gentry had the right to vote.

The gasworks that had once stood on the site had been known to all woodland and countryside animals since time-in-memorial, which was in fact, since it had been built in the late 19th century but then the gasworks had been demolished shortly after the discovery of North Sea natural gas in the mid 20th century and an underground grid pipeline had been laid throughout the whole of the country to distribute natural gas nationwide. Coal gas had become far too expensive to produce simply because its production depended on cheap supplies of coal. The cost of transporting coal by pack ponies had been the only means of getting coal to the gasworks and had made the processing of coal gas extraction financially uneconomical.

The gasworks too had also become obsolescent through age. Maintenance costs to continue working it as a commercial undertaking also made it economically non-viable. The old dilapidated *public utility* company had become expendable, as too had the pack ponies that had brought coal to the gasworks site from coalfields on the far side of the county. It was, in fact, pack pony convoys that had created the animal tracks leading to and from the gasworks site, to the pitheads of the coalmines. A broad two-way track that had been no more than a simple bridle path before it came to be used by generations of pack ponies, lugging heavy loads of coal to the gasworks and coke to the steel works.

When the gasworks closed down, the pack ponies were made redundant. They were rewarded for a lifetime of devoted service with a small lump sum *ex-gratis* severance payment. That was because they had been employed as sub-contracted hauliers to Animal Country Parkland Borough Council through 'Schemers Employment Agency Limited'. Schemers Employment Agency was a sub-contracting personnel agency, an employment subsidiary company of Reynard's and Serpents Civil Engineering and Construction Company Limited. The pack ponies' sub-contracted employment by an employment agency was a simple ruse that was used to bar them from receiving monies under the Redundancy Payments Act and also to preclude them from being entitled to join or benefit in any way from Animal Country Parkland Borough Council's staff pension fund.

As a direct result of the gasworks closure, after the pack ponies were made redundant they had neither a wage nor a pension as income. What little savings they had been able to accumulate from their low wages for lugging coal to the gasworks and coke to the steel smelters all their working lives was soon spent. They had all become sullen and depressed at being made unemployed and unemployable due to their age and lack of basic education or any other skills, and with no regular wage or income to sustain them other than at poverty level, their personal pride drove them to move away from their beloved Animal Country Parkland; a place they loved and that had been the pack ponies' country abode for hundreds of years. So they moved to the New Forest and to Dartmoor, where they were allowed to roam free and unmolested as *tourist attractions* in their unwanted but well-earned retirements, till their dotage. But as they all knew, in the course of time a knacker would be called on to come and claim their mortal remains.

However, it was several years after the gasworks had been closed down, (to all intents and purposes it had been abandoned), and most of the plant and other equipment had been destroyed by local vandals or stolen by wandering 'yeggs' out scavenging for easily removable non-ferrous metals and other valuable items and, after several young animals had been attacked while playing on the site, council officers who had inspected the area at the behest of the council's Senior Executive Officer, Mr Grass Snake, (better known to all those animals that knew him as Mr 'Slippery'), the site was declared unsafe and dangerous to innocent trespassers, wanton vandals and itinerant thieves who, if they were injured in or around the deserted buildings, may sue the borough council for compensation. Sly-Fox, (with a wink at the Senior Executive Officer), therefore agreed that Mr Grass Snake should take immediate and appropriate action to render the site safe by whatever means were necessary.

It was therefore put on record that on the council officer's recommendation, the borough council's Senior Executive Officer had advised the elected councillors that the gasworks site should be cleared of all of its previous industrial installations. It was a decision that was made during a full borough council meeting and entered in the minute book and that the Senior Executive Officer, Mr Grass Snake, shall also make all necessary contractual arrangements for that order to be carried out.

The London (Animal) Gazette, national and local newspapers, published on behalf of Animal Country Parkland Borough Council, an open offer to demolition companies to tender for contracts to demolish the gasometers, gas retorts, coal tar tanks and all other physical structures down to ground level; for the clearance of all stone, brick rubble, cast iron and steel, non-ferrous metals - brass, copper and gun-metal, asbestos insulation, fabrics and all other debris from the redundant gasworks site.

A tender for the 'overall' contract for the site clearance was accepted by the Animal Country Parkland Borough Council from British and Overseas Animals Demolition Company (Gibraltar) Limited. It was a company recommended by Councillor Sly-Fox, even though its submitted tender was among the highest placed before the council's Tenders Selection Committee; a committee that was advised by the borough council's Senior Executive Officer, Mr Grass Snake. The tender was accepted even though it was known to be a subsidiary company of the infamous RASCELS. RASCELS then arranged a sub-contract with British and Overseas Animals Demolition Company (Ireland) Limited, to demolish the buildings and then sub-contracted the job of clearing the site to Carry-all Transportation Services (Cayman Islands) Limited, yet another of RASCELS subsidiary companies, which then arranged for the hundreds of tons of scrap steel and non-ferrous metals to be recovered off the gasworks site, which was directly at the side of M A tracks, to various steel and non-ferrous metal smelting companies for re-processing; these were companies in which RASCELS held substantial share holdings.

The hardcore of stone, brick rubble and asbestos corrugated roof panels from the demolished buildings that had no immediate intrinsic value, had never left the old gasworks site. It was instead, spread over and pummelled into pre-selected areas of reclaimed land, to a depth of one metre, (so it was said), to act as hard standing to accommodate heavy horse-drawn transport, civil engineering equipment and other industrial plant belonging to Reynard's and Serpents Civil Engineering and Construction Company Limited, in spite of the fact that the A track leading onto the site led off the busy M A track; a track that had been reinforced and resurfaced at the expense of the county council's and borough council's rate payers, by International Road Resurfacing (Cayman Islands) Limited, a subsidiary company of British and Overseas Demolition Company (Gibraltar) Limited, for the sole purpose of transporting the thousands of tons of metals, brick hardcore and stone rubble off the old gasworks site.

Originally, when the gasworks site had been cleared, the contractors without having been given any form of written legal consent by the Animal Country Parkland Borough Council, had had the temerity to remain on site, using the hard standing that company itself had put in place, to park and repair its heavy construction plant and equipment on the pre-prepared hardcore base. A very substantial fence was installed around the whole area of the demolished gasworks site and there RASCELS sub-contractor's equipment was permitted to stay, rent and rate free, for twelve years, unmolested and unchallenged by the borough council's Senior Executive Officer, 'Slippery' Grass Snake, nor any of the other elected councillors. Even when RASCELS had claimed 'squatter's rights' of the land, there was no opposition from the borough council's Legal Department. So, without any opposition, the redundant gasworks site was duly transferred to Reynard's and Serpents Civil Engineering and Construction Company Limited by the Land Registrar's Office, under powers conferred on it by the Law of Property Act, 1925.

Councillor Sly-Fox had been, before his retirement, Chairman of British and Overseas Animals Demolition Company (Gibraltar) Limited. He was also one of its major shareholders before taking *early retirement* with an undisclosed lump sum, a 'diamond handshake', that was said to have run into seven figures; a lump sum payment that had been paid into the Bank for Tax Evading Animals (Swindleland) Limited. He had also accumulated a substantial long-term company pension, the lump sum from which, for tax evasion purposes, was also paid into the Bank for Tax Evading Animals (Swindleland) Limited by RASCELS (Gibraltar) Limited. If challenged as to whether he had any further dealings with his former company, he would vehemently deny such assertions. He would stress that he no longer (ostensibly) sat on its board or had any connection or dealings with that company or its businesses.

Soon after his arrival in Animal Country Parkland, Sly-Fox gave an interview to Ms Nosey Parrot, (a reporter for 'The News of the Weald'), at his mansion 'The Lair'. During the interview he claimed it had always been an ambition of his to serve his local community as a councillor and perhaps some time in the future, if nominated by his party's Parliamentary Selection Committee, to be the elected representative for Animal Country Parkland in the House of Common Animals. On the strength of the publication of the interview, Sly-Fox had been duly elected, almost immediately, onto the Animal Country Parkland Borough Council by undereducated, unread, politically ignorant animals, based on his promise to 'make Parklands a fit and safe place for all animals to live in'. Then, because of his *vast knowledge* of and close *past contacts* within the civil engineering and construction industry, he was automatically nominated by fellow party member, Councillor Venomous Viper, JP, to be the Chairman of the Planning and Construction Committee.

So, when it was proposed by Councillor Venomous Viper, JP, at a meeting of the Planning and Construction Committee that a new school was required to facilitate the education of a growing, young animal population in the area and, as human beings were moving into the countryside at an alarming rate and taking over the land and building houses on all the best development sites available in the countryside and, that all the small animals were being driven more and more onto wasteland considered to be unfit for human habitation, what better animal to be in charge of 'Planning and Construction' projects than Councillor Sly-Fox. Also, what better location was there to build a school other than on the brown field site known locally as 'the wreck' but the former gasworks site that lay on the opposite side of a busy M A track, close to the residential housing estate it was to serve.

Of course, it took several sessions at the borough council's Planning Committee meetings of discussions to take place as to the viability of the proposal for a primary school to be built on the former gasworks site. For, as Councillor Sly-Fox had fervently pointed out to the committee in a statement that he insisted on being documented in the Planning and Construction Committee's *minutes of the meeting,* "The top layer of soil on the gasworks site had been discovered as being contaminated with arsenic, heavy metals and other dangerous and noxious substances; substances that *shall have to be removed* before any building work may be allowed to commence on the site." Councillor Sly-Fox went on to state, "I am positive that with my numerous contacts within the civil engineering and construction industry, amicable arrangements regarding the cost of removing the offending soils from the site can be obtained, making the site safe for any future development work to be carried out." He then turned his head as he gave a crafty smile to Councillor Venomous Viper, JP, and winked at Mr 'Slippery' Grass Snake.

It was on this 'guaranteed assurance' from Councillor Sly-Fox stating the job of clearing the offending noxious, toxic chemicals and heavy metals could be safely removed, that contracts were tendered for part of or the whole of the proposed school development plan. The contract included the design for a new school, its playing field and play grounds. It came as no great surprise to anyone, especially the older inhabitants of Animal Country Parkland, when the contract was awarded to Councillor Sly-Fox's previous employer, whose address was given as:

Reynard's and Serpents Civil Engineering and Construction Company Limited, The Old Gasworks Site,

M A track Junction,
Animal Country Parkland

However, it took several re-appraisals of the contract, at the request of British Animals Overseas Demolition Company (Gibraltar) Limited, to take into account anomalies that were expected to occur during the clearing of the gasworks site and the construction of school buildings, such as the likelihood of *'bees, beavers and donkeys striking for higher wages, and safer working conditions'* and *'constructive work alterations'* that may be required and *'wet weather stoppages that were expected to occur during construction of the school'*. The borough council was advised by Councillor Sly-Fox, after consultation and advice from the borough council's Senior Executive Officer, 'Slippery' Grass Snake that the borough council should agree to a new clause in the 'terms and conditions of the contract' under which the proposed primary school shall be built.

Once a new contract had been approved, work was quickly commenced and when the site was said to have been cleared of all offending surface contamination, foundations were laid to meet with council approved building regulations and specifications (that followed the perimeter outline of the hardcore previously laid as 'hard standing' for the heavy mechanical plant equipment owned by RASCELS). It was 'hard standing' that was now to be used as the permanent oversite for the inner floor of the new school, even though the contaminated earth beneath the rubble had not been cleared.

School buildings were quickly erected over the pre-prepared oversite, play and sports areas were put in place and, when the work was finally finished, (there was a short overrun of several weeks in the completion of the school due to it was said 'unforeseen subsidence' and the hold-up cost the borough council a further several million pounds of rate payer's money), the school was opened to a fanfare of trumpets at which all the town councillors, county councillors, county 'big-wigs' and their invited guests were in attendance.

His Worship the Mayor, Councillor Gobbler Turkey and his Mayoress, Her Worship Mrs Trotter Turkey, JP, both of whom looked resplendent in their official regalia and gold chains of office were there in their official capacity. There was also My Lord Cock-of-the-Hoop Peacock, Lord Lieutenant of the County, prancing hither to and thro' flashing his resplendent tail feathers that showed all the colours of a rainbow. He was accompanied by his pretty but plainly dressed wife, Lady Peahen Peacock, both of whom mingled freely among the nobs, toffs, snobs, swells and elected borough councillors, together with their wives/partners/companions and numerous cohorts of council officials, some of whom were wearing medals, insignia or both. The females among them were covered in various forms of trumpery or dressed in mantles of glutinous furs, (as was Ms Mink), or drab feathers with brightly covered trinkets, (as was Mrs Magpie), and/or silky skin, (as was Mrs Grass Snake), who swanned or slithered about the new school buildings and play areas, each one trying to outdo the other in their garishness.

It was a display of pomp and pomposity that would have gone unnoticed by the general animal population had it not been for a freelance newspaper photographer who appeared to have been enchanted by the spectacle and sold his photographs of the event to 'The News of the Weald', an idea suggested to him by none other than Sly-Fox.

But to most of the other animals that lived their precarious lives in Animal Country Parkland, all this pretentious magnificence signified *absolutely nothing*. Nothing that is except for the *snobbishness and the airs and graces* of those gluttonous animals as they were photographed gorging themselves on cucumber sandwiches, hors-d'oeuvre, sausages on sticks and numerous other delicacies and relishes, that disappeared off plates as fast as the penguin waiters could replace them and who drank champagne as fast as the wine waiters could refill their glasses. All this frivolousness was at the expense of the animal rate payers of Animal Country Parkland, none of whom had been invited to the new schools grand opening. Then, finally to conclude the event, Lady Peahen Peacock, the invited Guest of Honour, was asked by His Worship the Mayor if she would cut the ribbon that was strung between the new school gates and who while doing so declared in a slightly inebriated voice, "I declare this Primary- *Hic-*School for Young Animals opened." However, to save any embarrassment to Her Ladyship, the school was thereafter known to all and sundry as 'The Primary *High* School for Young Animals'. It was a name that was in educational or any other jargon for that matter, a contradiction in terms.

After the Primary *High* School had been officially opened by Lady Peahen Peacock, the Lord and Lady Peacock returned to their residence at 'The Peacocks Gables Farm', a secure, guarded, isolated establishment with CCTV cameras and guard dog security patrols to ward off any intruders. It was a refuge from where they would not be seen again in public having to mix with those *other* obnoxious nobs, toffs, snobs, swells and borough councillors, till the opening of some other public facility. It was at this country residence too, where the Lord and Lady Peacock's children were privately educated. They were taught each day by a visiting 'tutoring governess', who was none other than Mrs Sly-Fox, a sharp-snouted, bushy tailed, red coated vivacious vixen, whose specialist educational teaching subjects were classical cunning, perverted deviousness, woodland stealth and self preservation; four of the major countryside disciplines in which she herself had graduated from the University of Life with First Class Honours degrees. These skills she passed on to the Peacock offspring, so they should grow up to appreciate their hereditary superiority over all the small, timid, state educated animals that lived in Animal Country Parkland.

PART 2

The Rebellious Mothers
of the Young Animals that attended
The Primary *High* School

"I've had enough of this,' said Mrs Slow, the tortoise, to her twin daughters Ambling and Dawdling Slow. "Trying to cross these animal tracks during the rush hours, with Greyhounds and Whippets dashing about, Poodles speeding by with their noses in the air, Saint Bernards and Great Danes lumbering back and forth along the animal tracks racing each other like demented demons – far exceeding the speed limit, it really is getting beyond a joke. You children have to be taken to school but with all due respect to the planning authority, why on earth did the local council build a school on the opposite side of a busy A track to our residential parkland housing estate?"

"The answer to that question," butted in Mrs Prickly Hedgehog, who had been listening to the conversation, "is that RASCELS, when Councillor Sly-Fox was the Chairman of that company, donated the site that it had claimed by *squatter's rights* to Animal Country Parkland Borough Council. That generous gesture was made specifically on the single condition that the site was to be used for educational purposes only. Of course, Sly-Fox knew the land was on the wrong side of the animal tracks for a school to be built. He must know too, from personal experience, that those canines - Greyhounds, Whippets, Poodles, Saint Bernards and Great Danes - nor any other of those other big, fast moving animals using the M A tracks, have any respect for pedestrians such as the likes of we other animals, not even at school crossings. One has to question the motive for Sly-Fox's benevolence in giving the gasworks site that his company had claimed by 'squatter's rights' when he was the Chairman of RASCELS, back to the borough council. After all, Sly-Fox and his colleagues have never been known for their philanthropy. They're not known as RASCELS for nothing you know."

"No," replied Mrs Slow, "poor Mrs Dormouse, the lollipop lady, has often had to throw herself clear of the pedestrian crossing when some of the big dogs deliberately ignore her lollipop sign. She told me that on several occasions, she has reported some of the large animals to the police but all she gets told is that "Unless an animal should be killed or injured, there is nothing very much we can do about it."

There were angry murmurs of agreement from all the other young animal's mothers who were waiting to cross the A track with their offspring and who had been listening in on the conversation. This included Mrs Snail, who was always first to start crossing the animal track and the last to get to the other side of it, in either direction. That was till Mrs Tortoise suggested she would carry Mrs Snail and her children on her back across the animal track, for even though that precaution wasn't much faster, at least it was just that little bit safer for her and her offspring.

However, it was Mrs Mole who had to be led across the M A track each day because of her poor eyesight that came up with the first suggestion to alleviate the problem. She raised herself up onto her short, fat, powerful hind legs and shouted above the other angry mother's conversations,

"Let's all march to the Town Hall and demand to see our local borough councillors and insist they represent us in forcing the council to come up with a solution to this M A track crossing problem. I've already spoken with Mrs Sly-Fox, Councillor Sly-Fox's wife, and to my husband about this dangerous M A track crossing on several occasions. Neither of them can see any reason why the council cannot have a tunnel built under the M A track. Do any of you?" shouted Mrs Mole, raising her voice above the protestations of all the young animal's mothers. (Mr Mole, better known as Digger Mole, was an expert tunnelling engineering consultant. He was also a sub-contractor to RASCELS and obviously would have a vested financial interest in the construction of a tunnel, should it be decided by Animal Country Parkland's Borough Councillors to vote for such a facility to be excavated beneath the M A track into an area close to the school).

Mrs Mole's last question and suggestion was brought to a short, sharp conclusion, when Mrs Badger yawned loudly. (It was passed her bedtime as she worked on the nightshift in Parkland's Coroner's office with her husband). Then she butted into the arguments that had been getting noisier and angrier as the young animal's mothers began to build up resentment against those in power, towards those councillors whose *apparent* lack of forward planning and consideration for the small common taxpaying animals had brought about this rowdy and rebellious situation.

"We shall have to force our way across the M A track en-block," ordered the usually shy but fearless Mrs Badger, "follow me!" So all the animals acting as one large group pushed their way onto the M A track, forcing the larger animals to stop and let them cross. It was an act that brought howls of rage, yelps, snarls, growls, barks and threats of physical violence from the furious dogs towards the mothers and their children. The canines were deterred from taking any form of violent action by Mrs Badger when she turned to face them, bared her teeth and snarled back at them.

After having crossed the road and seen their children safely into school, the mothers retreated back across the M A track by the same route they had come but now they were more determined than ever in their endeavour to

get a safe crossing to the school. They then marched en-block on the council offices at the Town Hall and demanded to see their locally elected councillor, Councillor Sly-Fox. When they asked the desk clerk at the council office for a consultation with Sly- Fox, Ms Snappy Yappy, a short haired, short tempered, short stumpy-legged brown and white coated Yorkshire Terrier, who was employed by the borough council as a front desk receptionist clerk, snapped at them, "You can't see your elected council representative until the next full council meeting is in session."

"When is that likely to be?" Mrs Slow, the tortoise, asked.

"I haven't been notified of the next full council meeting yet. You will have to contact the Town Hall through our 'website' sometime next week for that information," she 'yapped-yapped' at them. "The Chairman of Planning and Construction, Councillor Sly-Fox, is away on urgent business at present. He will not be available till later in the week." Then, when the young animal's mothers turned to file out of the foyer, she loudly 'yapped-yapped' officiously after them,

"And close the door on your way out!" she ordered.

As the mothers trooped out of the council's building in an orderly line, Mrs Badger who was last in line and the rear guard turned and smiled at Ms Snappy Yappy. Then, deliberately raising and wiggling a hind leg, she walked slowly out of the building, stopped to smile back at Ms Snappy Yappy again, before slamming the door shut behind her with a resounding crash.

Once outside the council offices and during a short discussion as to what should be their next move, the young animal's mothers agreed to meet outside the Town

Hall every morning after taking their children to school, and chant,

"*We want a school crossing! We want a school crossing! A crossing, a crossing, a school crossing!*" till Councillor Sly-Fox should choose to come and talk to them. But the following day when the young animal's mothers were once more standing beside the M A track waiting for an opportunity to crossover with their offspring, Mrs Mole again raised herself up on her short, fat, little hind legs and shouting above the constant noise of the big animals racing up and down the busy M A track, barking and snarling at each other, explained to the assembled mothers,

"I told my husband what had transpired yesterday when we went to the council offices to ask for a consultation with our elected representative and how we had been fobbed off by the council's front desk receptionist clerk, Ms Snappy Yappy. He was furious and telephoned Councillor Sly-Fox, who he knew was attending an important meeting at the 19th Green of his golf club. Sly-Fox was very angry at the way we had been treated by Ms Snappy Yappy and Digger Mole, my husband, said that Councillor Sly-Fox was very receptive to *his* suggestion, that a tunnel is required for the young animals to be able to cross the M A track in safety in order to get to school."

"What happened then? What else did Sly-Fox say?" said Mrs Slow.

"Sly-Fox said he had already contacted his party political colleagues on the Planning and Construction Committee about this problem," continued Mrs Mole, "and after discussing the proposal about the need for some form of crossing under or over the M A track with his councillor colleagues and, after having also taken advice from the directors of RASCELS, (Messrs Foxy–Fox, (the son of Councillor Sly-Fox), Venomous Viper, Cant Polecat, Holster Ferret and Willy Weasel), Councillor Sly-Fox intimated he was of the opinion that a tunnel may be the best solution to our problem relating to a safe crossing to the new Primary *High* School. He also said the council would have to keep all options open as to the type of crossing. That means all options relating to its structure and costs would have to be examined and mutually determined when the matter comes up for discussion at a full meeting of the council's Planning and Construction Committee. Such a costly construction proposal would have to be given a great deal of consideration before being passed over to the council's Planning Officers, who would then be responsible for drawing up the necessary lists of contract tender submissions and costing relating to the request for an M A track crossing. It shall then be looked into as a priority project in the immediate future."

It was then that Mrs Squirrel butted in on the debate, "A tunnel! Why a tunnel? Why not a bridge?" she asked.

"Because," replied Mrs Mole, "a tunnel is far more cosmetically friendly and unobtrusive in the countryside."

"Yes and far more dangerous to we smaller animals," interjected Mrs Rabbit.

"I agree with Mrs Mole for demanding a tunnel," shouted Mrs Stoat, licking her lips. Then she said, "What about you, Mrs Weasel?"

"Yes, I'm all for the idea of a tunnel," replied Mrs Weasel, winking at Mrs Polecat.

During this time the other young animals had kept silent but soon there was some dissention among them as they weighed up the pros and cons of the situation. Since her last outburst, Mrs Squirrel had stayed silent. Now she broke into the heated debate that was going on.

"I say we need a bridge," said Mrs Squirrel. "Tunnels are dangerous places for young animals, as Mrs Rabbit has just said. At least with a bridge one can see and be seen. I'll never use a tunnel to take my children to school, never. I'd sooner go on crossing the animal track, it's far safer."

"Mrs Squirrel is quite right," said Mrs Dormouse, stroking her whiskers, "but we shall have to wait and see what Councillor Sly-Fox recommends when we meet him and his councillor colleagues, won't we?"

"No, we shall not!" replied Mrs Squirrel, pawing her face. "Councillor Sly-Fox is our elected representative on the borough council. We should tell him straight to his face that, if he wants our support in the forthcoming elections, it is in his best interests to get a safe crossing put over the M A track."

"Or under it!" screamed out the Mesdames Mole, Stoat, Polecat, Ferret and Weasel in complete harmony.

Having agreed to meet with the mothers, whose offspring now attended the *Primary High School for Young Animals* and having been told by the mothers at that meeting if he wanted their votes then he had better arrange for a 'safe crossing' to be built over or under the M A track before the next borough council elections, Sly-Fox hastily called an emergency meeting of his political party's representatives on the borough council and told them of his intention to consult together with the Directors of RASCELS. (He had previously lied to Digger Mole when he told him that he had already spoken to his councillor colleagues and the construction company's representatives to discuss with them the M A track crossing problem). Sly-Fox then arranged a second meeting to be held at the 19th Green golf clubhouse with the Bridge Club Committee, a secret organisation that manipulated, among many other corrupt operations in which it was involved, the exploitation of civil engineering and construction contracts and in which it had agents employed on every conceivable major construction site operating throughout the western world.

The Bridge Club Committee was a separate membership from that of the golf club and met in the 'Life Members Only' boardroom, a luxurious suite where Reynard's, Serpents and Stoats Families Trust carried out their covert business meetings. Membership of the Bridge Club Committee was limited to selected personages, deemed to be wealthy, supposedly worthy too but who were, most certainly, influential and corruptible co-conspirators. They either lived within the borough's boundaries with business in the borough or had vested interests in the business of the borough but lived outside the borough; or, businesses that extended beyond the borough boundaries that could be manipulated for the financial benefit of Reynard's, Serpents, Stoats and Weasels Engineering and Construction Company Limited, which was the major holding company nationally and worldwide and too, the individual club members themselves. The golf club's Bridge Club Committee consisted of:

Councillor Sly-Fox, Chairman; Councillor Venomous Viper, JP, Vice-Chairman; Willy Weasel JP; Ms Ermine-Stoat, secretary, Deputy Mayor Councillor Dipper Magpie, JP; senior Superintendent Sniffer Blood Hound, the borough's Chief of Police and 'Slippery' Grass Snake, the borough council's Senior Executive Officer. There was also an American and a Canadian present, each of whom represented its stoat and weasel cousins from their two respective countries.

The American and Canadian were known to the rest of the committee members present at the meeting, as Fetid (Smelly) Skunk and Vic (short for Vicious) Mink, animals that 'for the right price' or 'for political expediency' or 'on the orders of the Bridge Club Committee', would get things done by whatever method or means *they* considered necessary.

There was also an Honorary Member of the Bridge Club Committee who, for personal and security reasons, never attended its meetings but was kept informed of all relevant decisions pertinent to his Honorary Membership function. He was, of course, the Member of Parliament for Animal Country Parkland, whose sole function as an Honorary Member of The Bridge Club Committee was to represent the interests of Reynard's, Serpents, Stoats and Weasels Civil Engineering and Construction Company Limited in the House of Common Animals. It was, in fact, none other than Black Rat QC, MAP, who always received a 'tasty fat fee' for his *benign* representations, (but not illegal or criminal services), to the Bridge Club Committee, as such shenanigans were an acceptable perk of elected members of the House of Common Animals. They were well paid services that were placed before those of his duty to his constituents, which was unless they dovetailed over a prominent local issue, such as an under-pass or bridge to be constructed under or over the M A track into the school for young animals.

Black Rat QC, MAP, had been forewarned by Sly-Fox that there may be some social unrest in Animal Country Parkland and unless the safe crossing currently being proposed for the construction under or over the M A track into the Primary *High* School for Young Animals was implemented, instigated by the young animal's mothers who had threatened Sly-Fox with voting against him at the forthcoming borough council elections. So, Black Rat was informed it was of paramount importance that such a scheme was put in place with some urgency and that parliamentary approval may be required and an exchequer grant needed to facilitate the building of a crossing. When he had been informed of this, Black Rat sat up on his hindquarters and thoughtfully stroked his whiskers as he looked forward eagerly to receiving his usual 'tasty fat fee' for his services should they be called on.

All Bridge Club Committee meetings were held in the 'Life Members Only' suite at the 19th Green clubhouse, known to the golf club members as the Bridge Room because it straddled a fast flowing stream. It was a sound-proofed room specially built over a stream, which had purposely had large misshaped rocks placed in it directly beneath the Committee Room so that the artificially created rippling waters would defuse any sound detector equipment that may be used by nosey media investigative reporters, more specifically, those working for 'The News of the Weald', to listen in on covert planning, costing, tendering or retributive (physical or monitory) operations that were under discussion. In other words, it was only used for highly confidential Bridge Club Committee meetings such as membership selections and convoluted discussions on policy procedures that were to be carried out and where too, cartel formulas between companies supposedly vying for various contracts (in this case, the proposed school underpass) were set in motion well before an official request for the submission of 'plans and costs' of the crossing was opened to all interested parties inviting them to submit tenders for the contracts.

The scheme and objective of the plan was therefore that most tenders would be more costly than that submitted by RASCELS or any other of the companies within its group of companies that had been chosen to apply for and obtain the contract. Each of the 'contract submissions' was in fact, a stitch in the fabric of deceit that had been formulated by the Bridge Club Committee in order to obtain for its controlling company a lucrative and highly prized contract - a contract that Councillor Sly-Fox and the council's Senior Executive Officer 'Slippery' Grass Snake of Animal Country Parkland Borough Council would connive together to gain by any means.

When the meeting was declared open, Councillor Venomous Viper, JP, immediately began to ingratiate him to Sly-Fox. He congratulated Councillor Sly-Fox on his handling of the 'squatter's rights land grab', for manipulating the 'gasworks demolition site contract', for the very lucrative extra income obtained from the salvaged steel, cast iron and non-ferrous metals sold on to metal processing companies and for the 'site clearance contract relating to hardcore and rubble' that had been deftly left on site, initially as hard standing for the companies' heavy construction equipment but purposely as the base for a primary school that had not, as yet, been conceived by the borough councillors, with the exception, that is, of the borough council's Senior Executive Officer, 'Slippery' Grass Snake, who worked in tandem with Sly-Fox.

Venomous Viper, JP, also congratulated Sly-Fox on his foresight in gaining control of the 'gasworks' site through 'squatter's rights law'. (A coup Sly-Fox had to admit, giving the slyest of sly looks and a wink in 'Slippery' Grass Snake's direction, he could not have carried out without the connivance of 'Slippery' Grass Snake, the borough council's Senior Executive Officer). He congratulated Sly-Fox too, for his clever move in free-gifting the 'gasworks site' back to the borough council in order to obtain the school building contract and for the M A track resurfacing contract and, for this golden opportunity to snuffle up a school crossing contract, which included invitations for tenders to be submitted for a tunnel or a bridge, with the main emphasis being placed on a tunnel at the express request of the directors of RASCELS, who saw rich 'free meal ticket' pickings accruing from an underpass facility.

Finally, Venomous Viper, JP, proposed that the Bridge Club Committee should join him in giving a vote of thanks to Mrs Sly-Fox, specifically for the way she had, through psycho induced analytical mesmerism, (she brainwashed Mrs Mole with words), enticed Mrs Mole into acting as an unpaid, unsuspecting provocateur by stirring the young animal's mothers into demanding an M A track underpass into the new Primary *High* School for Young Animals. It was a statement that was met with, 'here, here' and 'she's a jolly good fellow and so say all of us' and other totally irrelevant and childish forms of superfluous endearments; in plain language, nonsensical verbal claptrap. A form of endearment ranting that always brought out the superfluous pomposity and arrogance of the speaker over the goodwill *supposedly intended* for the recipient of the verbosity; or in layman's language, the ranting of a pompous, ingratiating, corrupt, melodramatic, verbose gasbag. It was at this point in the proceedings that Sly-Fox called an end to the meeting, told Ms Mink to record the time then in his usual fashion he got up and without another word, exited from the room and was gone.

PART 3

Digger Mole, Wiggly Worm, and the feasibility pilot tunnel debacle

As predicted, the connived award of the new tunnel contract went to Reynard's and Serpents. It was a decision said to have been made by the Animal Country Parkland Borough Council's Planning and Construction Committee, with the confirmed approval of the Amenities Committee but in fact, it was a decision made by Sly-Fox and 'Slippery' Grass Snake, who convinced the other committee members that Reynard's and Serpents were the most experienced civil engineering company in underpass construction worldwide and were therefore the very best civil engineering organisation to construct an underpass crossing beneath the M A track.

Once the subway contract had been awarded to Reynard's and Serpents, Digger Mole was engaged as the sub-contractor to take charge of first cutting a 'pilot feasibility tunnel' under the M A track and into the school site before the main tunnel was opened up. Digger Mole was also ordered, by word of mouth from the site engineer in charge, Croaky Frog, who had been ordered by Sly-Fox – also by word of mouth - that the tunnel had to be dug out at the shallowest depth possible, so as to save money and increase profits by the site clearance sub-contractors not having to carry excessive amounts of sub-soil off site, (even though the 'blueprints' approved by the borough council stated the depth should not be less than 60cm). Sly-Fox also ordered that when the main tunnel was constructed, shallow shelves (with female facilities) would have to be cut in either side of the tunnel so that female glow-worms may be employed to light the tunnel from end to end.

"Female glow-worms?" Mole queried.

"Yes!" Sly-Fox told him, "because it's only female glow-worms that glow."

"Oh!" Mole replied in surprise, "I wasn't aware of that."

"No. With your poor eyesight that's understandable," Sly-Fox said with some sympathy and for once in his lifetime, he genuinely meant it.

Digger Mole was also *ordered* by Sly-Fox to sub-contract Wiggly Worm to cut a 'pilot feasibility tunnel' under the M A track before he himself began to excavate the main tunnel. So when they arrived at the tunnel site, Wiggly Worm began the task of wiggling his way into the earth after Digger Mole had dug a 55cm *deep cut* in the surface earth and sub-soil at what was to be the tunnel entrance. It was a deep enough cut that gave Wiggly Worm plenty of room to deposit the earth he excavated. Wiggly Worm, who was on a 'paid job and finish contract, payment on completion', initially sped off into the soft soil, 55cm below ground level but after several hours it was obvious something was amiss because no further excavated soil came out of the pilot tunnel entrance.

Digger Mole became concerned that Wiggly Worm was falling behind with his commitment under the terms of his contract but unsure as to what was happening inside the 'pilot feasibility tunnel', so he sent a web message to Slimy Slug, the borough council's Health and Safety at Work Officer who, just to be on the safe side of the law relating to the Health and Safety at Work Act, sent a web message to Reynard's and Serpents on site Civil Engineer, Croaky Frog, who wasn't on site at all but was reposed in his official off site office at Reynard's and Serpents head office in town, who in turn then webbed Digger Mole to ascertain what the problem might be. When he was told that what should be happening wasn't happening, he promised Digger Mole a substantial bonus payment for any extra work that may be necessary to enlarge the pilot tunnel and investigate what problems Wiggly Worm had encountered. Digger Mole quickly cut his way into the earth, following the line of the 'pilot feasibility tunnel' that had been excavated by Wiggly Worm.

It took some time for Digger Mole to reach the rear end of Wiggly Worm, who was lying stiff and still. He appeared to be dead but nevertheless, Mole managed to grip Wiggly Worm by his rear end and slowly draw him back to the tunnel entrance, where he lay prostrate. Wiggly Worm was completely motionless; no sign of a wiggle left in him. Dr Barn Owl was sent for and after examining Wiggly Worm, he had a short discussion with the lizard paramedic who had attended to him at the scene. He then pronounced Wiggly Worm to be dead. "Yes," he'd said, "he's well and truly dead."

Wiggly Worm's long rigor mortis body was put on an elongated stretcher, lifted onto the roof rack of an ambulance that was already on the scene and taken to the borough Mortuary where a post-mortem examination was later carried out by Dr Barn Owl, the Animal Country Parkland Borough Council's official Pathologist, who was to determine the cause of death. Dr Barn Owl then sent his report to the Coroner's office to inform the Coroner of the tragedy.

After all the preliminary work had been completed, two uniformed police hounds arrived on the scene, one of whom took a statement from Digger Mole.

PART 4

Mr Piebald Badger and the Coroner's Inquest

Following Dr Barn Owl's report on the death of Wiggly Worm, a Coroner's Inquest was arranged. Notifications to attend the inquest on Wiggly Worm were delivered by the Coroner's clerk, Constable Jack Daw, to those animals that were to be called as witnesses and those that had been selected to act as jurors. Thereby a Coroner's Court was duly convened. The Coroner, Mr Piebald Badger, resplendent in his black trousers, black and white jacket, sporting a bright black and white tie, entered his courtroom. Then, to an order from the court clerk of "All stand for Her Majesty's Coroner", Mr Piebald Badger sat down. The clerk then ordered those assembled in the courtroom to do likewise. The jurors were sworn in and then the Coroner turned to face the jury.

The jury was made up of several different animals, that included: two field mice; two woodland voles; two grey and two red squirrels; two hedgehogs; one tortoise and a large grumpy, snarling, ginger feral cat, who because of his aggressive, spiteful nature, was elected by his fellow jurors to act as the jury foreman.

"Now, you all know why you are here," said the Coroner to the jury, "it is to listen to the evidence surrounding the unfortunate death of the late Wiggly Worm. You will be asked at the conclusion of all the evidence given by witnesses, to arrive at a verdict. I shall be advising you on the making of that verdict. Do you all understand? Then let's get on with it," he growled. "Call Digger Mole to the witness box."'

Mole was the first witness to be called to give evidence. He came stumbling into the courtroom wearing his Sunday best; sleek black moleskin jacket with matching trousers, topped with a blue and white spotted neckerchief wound round his thick neck. He slowly grappled his way towards the witness box with the aid of a white walking stick, grabbed the witness box brass rails with his powerful dagger like claws and was sworn to 'Tell the truth, the whole truth and nothing but the truth' and to Digger Mole's reply of, "'I do," the Coroner continued.

"Now, Mr Mole, tell the court in your own words what actually happened on the day of this unfortunate accident."

"Well Sir, it were like this, Sir," replied Mole, "Wiggly Worm and me got to the place that had been designated by the council's Planning Department for the entrance to the new school access tunnel. First, I dug a *deep cut* in the surface topsoil to a depth of 60 cm that was so Wiggly Worm could remove the earth he excavated from the pilot tunnel into the cut; the tunnel was to be dug out at 55cms. The earth was moist and worked easily. Wiggly, that's what all us animals call him, quickly disappeared under the animal track. The excavated alluvial just seemed to be squirting out of the pilot tunnel, like toothpaste out of a tube. So I went off to get a cup of tea and a bite to eat. After all, Wiggly Worm didn't need my help. He knew his job of pilot tunnelling better than any other worm or mole alive today, so he did."

"How long were you away from the site, Mole?" the Coroner asked.

"I suppose I'd been gone away for about 'alf an hour. When I got back there was a huge pile of alluvial in the cut. I set about right away to clear it but once I had got it cleared, there weren't any more earth coming from out of the pilot tunnel. I thought maybe Wiggly Worm had resorted to his old 'abit of shoving the earth he'd dug-out up over his head and I was annoyed about that because if he had been doing that, there would have been worm mounds all over the surface above the tunnel and they have to be cleared away once the tunnel has been completed and that's an expensive job, that is, clearing up them worm mounds."

"But you moles always leave earth mounds when you have been excavating your tunnels, don't you?" Badger asked Mole.

"Well, yes we do Sir but only at the end of each run. We don't leave earth mounds willy-nilly all over the place, we don't. At least not like what untrained earthworms do, Sir," replied Mole.

"Yes, yes," replied Badger, "point taken but what action did you take then, Mole?"

"Well now, for the moment I was in two minds as to what I should do. Then I decided to send a message on the web and contact the borough council's Health and Safety at Work Officer, Slimy Slug."

"Oh, you did and what did Slimy Slug do?" Badger asked.

"What did Slimy Slug do, Sir?" repeated Digger Mole, "he didn't do anything, Sir. Slimy Slug told me it was far too dangerous for him to leave his office and come down to the tunnel site, as he may get injured himself but he did say he understood my dilemma and he sent a web message to Reynard's and Serpent's site engineer's office. That by the way is in the company's head office building in town," said Mole.

"Yes, yes. What did Reynard's and Serpent's on-site, off site engineer advise?"

"Well Sir," said Mole, 'I can't repeat what he said when I woke him up but when he came to, so to speak, the on-site, off site engineer asked me what the problem was. I told him Wiggly Worm was in the pilot tunnel and nothing was happening."

"So what did the on-site, off site engineer have to say to that?"

"He said, Sir, "I suppose the lazy devil has fallen asleep on the job. You'd better go in after him and if he is asleep, terminate his contract.""

"Then what did you say to the on-site, off site engineer on that score?"

"I told him Wiggly Worm wasn't like that, Sir. The sort of worm that fell asleep on the job. Then, after we'd had a short discussion as to an extra payment I should receive for my going into and widening the pilot tunnel, I went in following Wiggly Worm's trail till I found him. He was laying quite still when I came up behind him, so I took hold of his rear end and pulled him out of the tunnel into the deep cut I'd made earlier, Sir."

"Yes, yes. What happened then?" the Coroner asked impetuously.

"I got on the web and called Dr Barn Owl. He arrived and examined Wiggly Worm and pronounced him dead. That's about all I can tell you, Sir," said Mole.

"Not quite," replied the Coroner, "how far from the proposed exit opening on the far side of the M A track was Wiggly Worm when you found him?"

"About a metre, Sir," Mole replied.

"Did you shout to your colleague while he was in the tunnel?"

"No Sir, there was no point in doing that. Wiggly Worm's Mutton Jeff."

"Mutton Jeff, what do you mean by Wiggly Worm's Mutton Jeff?"

"Deaf, Sir, you know, Mutton Jeff - as in cockney rhyming slang Sir, deaf," said Mole. Then raising his voice he shouted, "Totally deaf, Sir!"

Dr Barn Owl broke into the Coroner's questioning of Digger Mole by saying,

"If you please Sir, Charles Darwin, the great English naturalist and author of 'The Origin of Species' carried out a number of biological experiments on earthworms to test if they had any audible senses. He even placed some worms on his wife's piano and had her play to them. Finally, after those tests he declared all earthworms to be totally deaf."

"What did the worms do when Mrs Darwin played her piano?" said Badger.

"They wiggled about just as earthworms do, Sir," said Dr Barn Owl.

"But couldn't the worms have been dancing to Mrs Darwin's music?"

"Not according to Charles Darwin's experiments with worms' audibility, that was why he pronounced that all earthworms are deaf, Sir. Totally and irrefutably deaf."

"So those experiments are accepted as being a scientific fact are they Dr Barn Owl?"

"Yes they are, Sir, and to my personal knowledge those experiments have never been disputed."

"I've just told him worms' is deaf," interjected Digger Mole, "that's why we Moles use worms to cut our pilot tunnels. What's more, they don't have to wear ear-protectors or use lighted helmets when they're working. Yes, earthworms are deaf all right, totally deaf, they're blind too," he said. Then, as Mole was about to leave the witness box, the Coroner said,

"Wait Mole, I've one more question. How far was Wiggly Worm's pilot tunnel away from reaching the far side of the M A track when you found him?"

"About a metre, Sir," replied Mole.

"Then why didn't you rescue Wiggly Worm from that end of the tunnel, Mole?"

"Why, Sir!" Mole exclaimed in utter surprise. "It was because my contract was to open a tunnel not to carry out a rescue operation. Nor would there have been any profit in opening the tunnel from the opposite side of the M A track. That, you see Sir, wasn't in the terms and conditions of my contract and on top of that, it may have offered me another business opportunity at some time in the future, when the tunnel had to be completed."

"Yes," said the Coroner, "but surely you have lost a dear friend and colleague. Had you have opened the tunnel from the far side of the M A track, you may have saved him?"

Mole looked dolefully up at the Coroner. He had large crocodile tears swelling up in the corners of his almost unseeing eyes when he said,

"In all truth, Sir, I knows I'll miss my faithful pilot tunnel cutter something dreadful. But fortunately at the moment there's a proliferation of Eastern European earthworms on the labour market looking for work. I've often caught them unemployed foreign worms sneaking into my tunnels, so I'll just have to catch one and train 'im as my new pilot tunnel cutter. It's a bit of a nuisance though at the moment 'cause I've got a lot of work on and it takes a lot of training to stop earthworms from pushing the alluvial they dig out of the pilot tunnels upwards but, the one consolation is them foreign worms are cheaper to employ. But as you know, Sir, worms is worms no matter where they come from and they all have this tendency to want to push soil up above the ground when they're working. That's probably because they all appear to suffer from what we moles call 'the *jelly baby* syndrome'."

"And what may I ask is 'the *jelly baby* syndrome' Mr Mole?" said Badger.

"It's a sort of St. Vitus's dance, Sir, a form of uncontrolled muscle spasms. You must know what I mean, Sir. The worms keep wiggling and twisting about, well that's when they're alive, that is." Then, as an afterthought, Mole said, "They don't wiggle and twist about when they is dead, Sir. At least, I've never seen 'em wiggle or twist about when they're dead. Not them worms I've not, Sir."

"No. Neither have I when I come to think of it," said Badger scratching his head as though trying to remember if he had or not. He then continued,

"Now, if there's nothing more you can tell me about this unfortunate accident, you may step down Mr Mole." Badger then ordered, "Call Slimy Slug to the witness box."

Slimy Slug slithered his way across the courtroom floor and into the witness box, leaving a trail of phosphorous slime behind him. Badger took out a pair of Pince-nez spectacles from his jacket pocket and glared down his snout at Slimy Slug then he said,

"Right Mr Slug, give the court your full name and qualifications."

"My name, Sir, is Slimy Slug. I hold a Health and Safety at Work Certificate (HSWC) and I am the current Health and Safety at Work Officer for Animal Country Parkland Borough Council."

"Yes, yes," said Badger. "Now, as I understand the situation from a previous witness, you were called on your website communications system by Mr Mole, the tunnel sub-contractor to Reynard's and Serpents and you were advised by him a worm that had been in the process of cutting a pilot tunnel under the M A track, in preparation for the building of an underpass to the new Primary *High* School, was stuck in the tunnel and that you refused to go to the new tunnel site to investigate the accident because, in your opinion, it was too dangerous for you to do so. Is that true?"

"Well, not exactly, Sir," fibbed Slimy Slug. "As I recall the incident, I was rather busily engaged at the time clearing up some rotting vegetables, although I do recall getting a message about something being referred to as dangerous but I can't remember if it was a tunnel or a funnel. It may even have been the rotting vegetable matter I was working on at the time that was being reported as construed as dangerous." Then as an afterthought, Slimy Slug said, "my website wasn't working very well at the time, Sir."

"Yes, yes, Mr Slug but the fact remains. You failed to attend the accident scene at the tunnel site and as

I understand from the evidence given by Mr Mole, you advised him to get in touch with Reynard's and Serpents tunnel site engineer. What was the purpose of that advice?"

"For Reynard's and Serpents site engineer to make the necessary arrangements to extricate the worm from the pilot tunnel, or funnel," replied Slimy Slug.

"Oh! I see," said the Coroner, "you thought at the time it was an engineering problem not a health and safety at work problem. That makes sense. Well now, Mr Slug, if there is nothing further you can help me with, you may slip down out of the witness box."

Slimy Slug slipped out of the witness box and retraced his passage back along the phosphorous trail he'd made previously. Then Badger ordered his clerk, after referring to his notes, to call Croaky Frog.

Croaky Frog, dressed in a black and brown jacket with yellow trousers covering his long legs, hopped across the Coroner's courtroom before jumping up into the witness box and focusing his large eyes on the Coroner.

"Please give your name, professional qualifications and a précis of your previous engineering experience to the court, Mr Frog," said the Coroner.

Croaky Frog sat in the witness box with his webbed feet gripping the witness box rail, his big hind limbs sticking up above his body and his large ears protruding out from behind his big eyes.

"I'm Croaky Frog, 'croak, croak - and croak'. I served in an Amphibious Engineering Company with the Royal Animal Electrical and Mechanical Engineers (RAEME) for twenty two years, 'croak, croak - croak'. I'm a Graduate Member of the Society of Amphibious

Animal Engineers. I'm currently in the employ of Reynard's, Serpents, Stoats and Weasels Civil Engineering and Construction Company Limited as the site engineer in charge of the M A track *underpass tunnel project* that is being built to give safe access into the Primary *High* School, 'croak, croak - croak'."

"Yes, yes, your credentials have been noted Mr Frog," said the Coroner. "Now then, explain to the court why you didn't deem it necessary to attend the tunnel site when Digger Mole sent you a web message telling you that Wiggly Worm had stopped work in the pilot tunnel he was excavating under the M A track."

"The answer to that question is simply that if Slimy Slug, the borough council's Health and Safety at Work Officer, didn't want to attend on account he might have got himself injured, 'croak, croak - croak', then there was no point in me leaving my warm, comfortable office to go to that muddy tunnel entrance. After all, Wiggly Worm was 'sub-contracted' to work for Digger Mole, Sir, 'croak, croak -croak'. Reynard's and Serpents have no direct contractual responsibility or legal liability for 'sub-contracted' employees. That's the reason why Reynard's and Serpents sub-contract to minor operators. There's no profit to be gained by accepting legal liability for all work employees on civil engineering sites. That is the responsibility of the sub-contractor employed to carry out the specified work and is laid down in the work contracts, 'croak, croak - croak'."

"Oh!" said Badger. "Now why is that?"

"Because there are always a goodly number of injuries and deaths in our line of business, Sir," replied

Croaky Frog. Then, after a short pause Croaky Frog continued, "Especially when we are contracted to excavate tunnels or to build bridges. We much prefer to employ specialist 'sub-contractors' to do those jobs for us. My company's motto on those jobs is 'let the *subby* take the strain; let the *subby* take the pain; let the *subby* take the blame', 'croak, croak - croak'."

"'Oh is it Mr Frog?" said Badger. "This court accepts your statement relating to the interpretation you place on the legal liability and responsibility for this accident. But the legal issue, as to whose responsibility the accident was due to, will no doubt be settled in the course of time under a common law claim. It will be a decision made by a Judge sitting in The High Courts of Justice, not your employers. You can be sure it will be one of His Majesty's Law Lords who decides who shall be held legally liable for the death of Wiggly Worm. I've no more questions for you, you may step down, or in your case Mr Frog, hop it."

When Croaky Frog had hopped out of the witness box, Badger called for Councillor Sly-Fox to take the stand, then changing his mind he asked,

"Did any paramedics attend the scene of the accident? I've not yet heard them mentioned. Can any animal in my courtroom shed any light on this?"

A police hound in the front row rose up on his front paws and said,

"I can help you here, Your Worship. It was I who took notes at the scene of the accident."

"Then you had better enter the witness box, Constable," Badger ordered. "Give your evidence from there."

The police hound rose slowly and laboriously off his well padded haunches onto his hind legs and even more slowly climbed into the witness box where he was told by Badger,

"Give your name, rank, number and police station address to the court, Constable."

"If it pleases Your Worship, Sir," the Constable replied, "I am Police Constable Beagle Hound number 3/34345, stationed at The Police Station, High Street, Animal Country Parkland."

"Yes, yes," said Badger, "but you do not need to call me 'Your Worship'. I'm not a Justice of the Peace. Now, tell me what happened in relation to anything you may have recorded relating to any paramedic activity at the tunnel site on the day of Wiggly Worm's demise."

"May I read from my notebook, Sir?" the Constable asked.

"Yes, yes of course, if it's relevant to this case," Badger said testily. "When did you make the notes?"

"Well, Sir, when I left the tunnel site and arrived back at the police station."

"That's OK then," said the Coroner. "Carry on Constable."

"Yes, Sir, right, Sir. It was at approximately 10.15 am after my having been ordered to attend the new tunnel site by the M A track. I should have left at 9.45 am but it was my tea break, Sir, so I didn't think a few more minutes would make much difference. I arrived at the tunnel site at 10.30 am by panda back, where I immediately noticed two paramedics trying to resuscitate an earthworm. The worm was lying prostrate on the ground, immediately outside what was to be the entrance to a new tunnel. One of the paramedics, who is known to me as Ms Lisa 'Luscious Lips' Lizard, was trying her 'kiss of life' resuscitation technique on the earthworm."

"What on Golly's earth is 'kiss of life' resuscitation, Constable? I'm intrigued," said Badger.

"It's a technique devised by a paramedic ambulance driver some years ago and taken to perfection by Ms Lisa Lizard, Sir. In Ms Lisa Lizard's case, the technique consists entirely of a 'mouth-to-mouth' lingering French kiss, Sir, with Lisa's 'Luscious Lips' covering over the whole of a patient's mouth, Sir. It's a great technique. Never been known to fail on any male animal that's got a spark of life left in it! Ms Lisa 'Luscious Lips' Lizard has perfected her art to such an extent, Sir, that it's said she could French kiss her lizard's tongue all the way down Wiggly Worm's mouth, almost to his rear end - and that's a long way to give anyone a French kiss, Sir. But them lizards do have long tongues, Sir. That's a well-known fact, that is. Every animal in the medical profession accepts that if a male patient doesn't respond to Ms Lisa's 'Luscious Lips' 'kiss of life' resuscitation technique, it must be dead," the Constable reported.

"Yes, yes, is that so. Then what happened next, Constable?"

"May I refer to my notebook again, Sir?"

"Yes, yes, if you must," replied Badger irritably. "Do get on with it."

"Right you are, Sir. Well, that's when Dr Barn Owl turned up. He bent down and made a preliminary examination of Wiggly Worm's body, put a mirror under his nostrils, got his stethoscope out and listened to see if there was a heartbeat. He then had a quiet word in private with Ms Lisa Lizard before he pronounced Wiggly Worm was dead."

"What happened after that, Constable?" said Badger.

"The ambulance crew put Wiggly Worm's body on a stretcher, lifted it onto a roof rack and took it to the hospital mortuary to be prepared for a post-mortem examination."

"Why did the ambulance crew put Wiggly Worm's body on a roof rack, Constable?" Badger asked in surprise.

"Because, Sir, when worms' is laid out when they're dead, they're very long, Sir. Now if rigor mortis sets in you just can't bend them about, Sir. They're like a stick of rock. Wiggly Worm's corpse was beginning to set hard and it was too long to fit inside the ambulance unless the rear doors of the ambulance were left open. Now it doesn't look very nice to see an ambulance going along the A track with a corpse sticking out of the back. That's why it had to be put up on the roof rack."

"'Oh! I see," said Badger, looking somewhat perplexed, "thank you for filling that gap in the evidence and in my education. If you've nothing more to add to your evidence you may now step down, Constable."

Badger then sat in silence for a few moments making notes. Then he looked up and said, "Right. Now I will hear evidence from Councillor Sly-Fox, if he would be so good as to step into the witness box and take the oath."

Sly-Fox, dressed in rust-red coloured trousers, white bib fronted shirt with chequered bow tie and a rust-red jacket, sauntered his way into the witness box where he rested one paw on the witness box brass hand rail before turning his head slowly towards the Coroner. Badger looked a bit perplexed but began to ask Sly-Fox in a very benign manner,

"Were you the Animal Country Parkland Borough Councillor responsible for setting in motion the contract to clear the gasworks site of toxic materials?"

"Yes, I was, Sir," replied Sly-Fox, rubbing his freshly manicured claws against his rust-red jacket before slowly turning his head to look about the courtroom.

"Was the former gasworks site, to the best of your knowledge, properly cleared of toxic material?" Badger asked.

"Oh yes, it was, Sir, absolutely. We councillors and council officers took our orders from the Medical Officer's of Health Department, after soil samples had been extracted from the site and analysed," replied Sly-Fox.

"Then how do you account for the unfortunate demise of Wiggly Worm, Sly-Fox?"

Sly-Fox gave one of his well-known cunning, sly looks around the Coroner's courtroom before he slowly and with smarmy deliberation replied,

"The contract awarded for the surface clearance of toxic waste from the former gasworks site did not extend beyond the former gasworks site boundaries and certainly not onto or beneath the M A track. That is a public secondary highway and comes under the jurisdiction of the County Highways Authority. It was, and is, the borough councillors' opinion that, even if they had known that there had been any seepage of dangerous waste substances away from the redundant gasworks site, which they most certainly did not, it didn't constitute a danger to the general animal population in our area of civic responsibility. Nor, may I add, would it have warranted the additional cost to the rate payers of this borough for a full exploratory assessment of toxic materials outside of the proposed school site area. That, too, is outside our area of responsibility and comes under the jurisdiction and is the responsibility of the County Highways Authority. The borough councillors of Animal Country Parkland were as shocked as the general public at the sad loss of Wiggly Worm and steps shall be taken, based on Dr Barn Owl's evidence to your good self, to see that such a shocking accident doesn't occur again. At least now that we have been made aware of those facts relating to the poisonous substances in the soil beneath sites previously used for industrial purposes."

"Then how do you and your council colleagues propose to overcome the problem associated with providing a safe crossing into the Primary *High* School for Young Animals?" said Badger.

"Simply by avoiding building a tunnel, at least until more research into the problem of toxic poisons has been overcome. In the meantime, we are looking at plans for the construction of a footbridge to be built over the A / M A road track junction as a simple alternative instead," Sly-Fox barked.

"Thank you for being so candid with your evidence, Sly-Fox," said Badger, "you may step down from the witness box, if you please." Sly-Fox made no reply, looked stoically round the courtroom with a smug look on his face and returned to his seat between Venomous Viper, JP, and 'Slippery' Grass Snake, who winked at him.

Badger looked up from his note-book and said, "Dr Barn Owl, please enter the witness box and prepare to give your evidence."

There was a flutter of feathers as Dr Barn Owl ruffled his wings, blinked his large brown eyes then flew silently to the witness box where he perched himself on the brass hand rail.

Badger, looking over his spectacles, then asked him politely,

"Please state your credentials Dr Barn Owl and then give the court your report on the autopsy you carried out on Wiggly Worm."

Dr Barn Owl perched himself comfortably on the witness box hand rail, blinked his large eyes several times, flapped his wings and puffed out his breast before saying,

"I'm Dr Barn Owl, *Professor of Pathology* at Animal Country Parkland General Hospital."

"Yes, yes," said Badger. "Now, if you will be so kind, please give the court a report on your findings of the post-mortem examination you carried out on the late Wiggly Worm."

"Yes, Sir," replied Barn Owl, "for as the court has already heard, I attended the deceased at the entrance to the proposed new tunnel site. I was met on site by one of my hospital's paramedic teams. They were at the scene of the accident before me and as I came to understand it, they had spent some time trying to revive the accident victim. Immediately on my arriving at the accident scene, I examined the victim where he lay, that was in the cut outside the tunnel entrance. I carried out all the normal and formal medical tests on the body but the victim, whose name I came to be informed of by his colleague, Digger Mole, was one Wiggly Worm. Mr Worm was already dead. Had been dead for some time and rigor mortis had began to set in. I ordered that the body should be taken to the 'public mortuary' and prepared for an autopsy examination. I left the supervision of transportation of the body to the ambulance crew and went about my other duties."

"Yes, yes," said Badger, "now would you be so good as to tell the court about your clinical findings. What was it that caused the death of Wiggly Worm?"

"I'll start by stating that other than those factors that caused Wiggly Worm's death, the victim was in good physical health. I noted from the beginning of my examination that the area round the worm's mouth was blue in colour. It was because of this I suspected the victim had died of lead poisoning. On my examination of the digestive system of the victim and on analysing the stomach contents, it showed Wiggly Worm had ingested large quantities of both lead and arsenic residue."

"For the benefit of the jury," interjected Badger, "you must explain to the court what effect these substances had on the deceased."

"Well, quite obviously, Sir, they killed him," replied Barn Owl.

It was a remark that quite unintentionally drew laughter from those assembled in the Coroner's courtroom.

"Don't be facetious, doctor. The court is well aware they killed him, otherwise why would we be here. But how did they kill him?"

"Very painfully and slowly I should think, Sir, as he ingested them as he was cutting his way along the pilot tunnel."

"Yes, yes, doctor but how?" Badger barked at him.

"Oh, Sir. I'm sorry, Sir," Barn Owl blurted out in embarrassment. He flapped his wings, blinked his eyes, re-adjusted his talons on the witness box rail and continued,

"Well, Sir, as the court is no doubt aware, all animals are different. For example, you yourself have a head, two eyes, two ears, a body, four legs, four paws and a tail. Whereas I, on the other hand, have a head, two large eyes, two pointed ears, a body, two legs with talons and wings. You, Sir, live underground but forage for food on the earth's surface near your burrow. I, on the other hand, live in a church tower well above the ground but I forage for my victuals some distance from my church clad ivy tower by the means of flight. Worms, on the other hand don't do any of these things. They live underground most of their lives and only come to the surface at night to feed on vegetation or during rainstorms when their tunnels get flooded, Sir.' Barn Owl took a sip of water and continued,

"Worm body components are different from other animals too. Their bodies are formed of rings, or annuli, that terminate in a pointed head at one end and a tapering tail at the other. Worms have no feet but on each ring are four pairs of minute bristles that form eight longitudinal rows, which assist their progression. Worms, as Charles Darwin discovered during one of his biology experiments into worm behaviour, have no gills. It would appear that they breathe through their skins. Worms are also blind and as you have already heard, Sir, deaf."

"Is that so?" interjected Badger. "I'd never realised worms had so many physiological setbacks. I think the court has mentally digested that most enlightening piece of information. Please continue your evidence doctor, by telling the court what it was that killed Wiggly Worm."

"Yes, thank you, Sir,' replied Barn Owl, "I was about to come to that. Wiggly Worm's death was the direct result of lead and arsenic poisoning. This occurred as he ingested earth beneath the M A track whilst digging a pilot tunnel for the proposed new subway crossing into the Primary *High* School. For the benefit of the court, arsenic is a chemical related to antimony and bismuth. In many respects it more closely resembles a non-metal, particularly phosphorus. Its atomic number is 33— atomic weight 74.96. Lead, on the other hand,"

"Stop right there doctor," said Badger. "I must put this question to you. Is there normally sufficient arsenic and lead in soil that will kill worms?"

"No, Sir, there is not. Arsenic does occur in nature seniorly as the sulphide orpiment realgar but the amount in the earth is generally not enough to kill. If it were, there would be no living animals left on this planet. Arsenic and its compounds, you see, Sir, are violently poisonous substances, as is lead. The sample of earth I took from Wiggly Worm's intestine and samples of earth I extracted from the pilot tunnel show conclusively that arsenic and lead had leached under the M A track from the former gasworks site.

"Yes, yes," the Coroner growled, "but what was the direct cause of Wiggly Worm's death, doctor?"

"As I have already categorically stated," Barn Owl hooted, "Wiggly Worm's death was due entirely to him having ingested large quantities of arsenic and lead, arsenic and lead which came from the soil he was excavating. In other words, soil from the pilot tunnel he was endeavouring to remove from beneath the M A track, Sir."

"Is there anything else you wish to add to your attestation, doctor?" Badger asked.

"No, Sir! That, Sir, concludes my evidence as it relates to the demise of Wiggly Worm. However, I feel it is my duty to inform you that the paramedic, Ms Lisa 'Luscious Lips' Lizard has been violently sick and ill since giving 'mouth-to-mouth' resuscitation to Wiggly Worm, as she tried to revive him on the day of his death. I thought you should be made aware of that fact, as she too is suffering from the effects of arsenic and lead poisoning."

"Ah! Then why isn't Digger Mole suffering from arsenic or lead poisoning doctor, when Wiggly Worm died from its effects and paramedic Lizard is only ill from its effects?" Badger questioned.

"Because moles only dig through the earth, they do not ingest earth as do worms. Lizards do not ingest earth. Miss Lizard's symptoms are due to her brave effort in trying to resuscitate Wiggly Worm by 'mouth-to-mouth' resuscitation, thereby coming into direct contact with those poisonous substances," Barn Owl hooted.

"Oh! I see," growled Badger, "but for the benefit of the jury, will you tell us what the difference is between ingestion and digestion?"

"Yes, certainly, Sir," replied Dr Barn Owl. "Ingestion means to take food into the body; digestion simply means the breaking down of the food that has been ingested."

"Well, doctor. Thank you for giving the court that extra piece of informative information. You may leave the witness box." Badger then sat scratching his head before turning to the jury and saying,

"On Dr Barn Owl's professional conclusion as to his medical findings, as they relate to the unfortunate death of Wiggly Worm, I direct you, the jury, to retire to consider your verdict. That verdict is to be based solely on the evidence given to this court by Mr Digger Mole, who was at the scene when the accident occurred and on the expert medical evidence given to this court by Dr Barn Owl. Do all you members of the jury understand what is required of you?"

"We understand," snarled Feral Cat, the jury foreman, as he led his colleagues out of the Coroner's courtroom into the jury room.

The jury were soon back in the jury box and the jury foreman informed the Coroner, which he read out from a written statement, that,

"We, the jury, find Wiggly Worm died from 'factors beyond present day animal control'. His death was due to ingesting then digesting large quantities of arsenic and lead during the course of his lawful employment as a tunnel pilot cutter, the employment being the *cutting of a 'feasibility pilot tunnel'* under an M A track. Our verdict is therefore 'Death by Misadventure'."

"Then 'Death by Misadventure' in the case of Wiggly Worm is the finding of this Coroner's court, so shall it be recorded," said Badger. He then added, "That concludes this Coroner's Inquest on the late Mr Wiggly Worm. However, I must point out that there can be no further work carried out on the proposed tunnel under the M A track till the problem of leaching poisons has been overcome. The County Highways Authority shall be advised of my decision forthwith. This court is now adjourned."

"All stand for Her Majesty's Coroner," ordered the court clerk, as Badger rose from his chair and disappeared through a door let in the wall at the back of the room.

PART 5

Sly-Fox's alternative
plan - a footbridge!

"Damn that accident," Sly-Fox was heard to say to Ms Nosey Parrot, a newspaper reporter employed by 'The News of the Weald'. "That means we shall have to apply 'Plan B' to our school crossing plan for the M A track."

"Oh!" Nosey Parrot exclaimed, "What is 'Plan B', Sly-Fox?"

"We shall have to give consideration to the building of a bridge, shall we not," he curtly replied. "That means we shall have to consult with the arachnids."

"What?" Nosey Parrot gasped, "Spiders!"

"Yes," Sly Fox replied through clenched teeth, "spiders!"

The following Sunday's headlines in 'The News of the Weald' read:

News scoop of the day, as reported by our Gossip Columnist, Ms Nosey Parrot.

Councillor Sly-Fox, Chairman of Animal Country Parkland Borough Council's Planning and Construction Committee, is to consult with Spiders International Limited for the design and building of a new footbridge over the M A track. A site has already been chosen for the footbridge that is to be built, which is to be over the M A track road access junction onto the former redundant gasworks site. This, Councillor Sly-Fox has stated, is because the borough council considers this to be the best site to give the public access to the new Primary *High* School. It is further understood by Ms Nosey Parrot, that a 'sub-contract' to build a footbridge is to be offered to Spiders International Limited by the main crossing contractor, Reynard's, Serpents, Stoats and Weasels, Civil Engineering and Construction Company Limited because Spiders International Limited is the sole holder of all the known patents relating to single span footbridge construction and, its bridging engineers are recognised throughout the world to be the foremost experts in this field of civil engineering technology. Councillor Sly-Fox, Chairman of Planning and Construction for Animal Country Parkland Borough Council, has issued the following statement,

"Animal Country Parkland Borough Council and its M A track contractor, Reynard's, Serpents, Stoats and Weasels, Civil Engineering and Construction Company Limited, are to make a joint approach to Spiders International Limited, as a matter of urgency, requesting them to accept an official 'sub-contract' for the design and construction of a single span footbridge over the M A track, at the notoriously dangerous M A track junction that leads to the Primary *High* School. This approach is to be made without Spiders International Limited having to submit a formal price costing tender."

"It is unfortunate this change in your council's plans has had to be made but in the light of the borough Coroner's verdict relating to the death of Mr Wiggly Worm in a pilot tunnel accident, the borough council has been left with no alternative but to abandon the tunnel project, for the time being at least, and to make alternative arrangements for a safe crossing to be built as quickly as possible over the M A track, for the benefit and use of those young animals who attend at the Primary *High* School on the former gasworks site."

However, Black Rat, QC, MHCA (Member [of the] House of Common Animals), when asked his opinion on Councillor Sly-Fox's statement with regards to a footbridge that was to be built by Spiders International Limited, made the following statement,

"I am of the opinion the informal approach to Spiders International Limited by the Animal Country Parkland Borough Council and Reynard's, Serpents, Stoats and Weasels, Civil Engineering and Construction Company Limited, with what can be described as an open cheque sub-contract offer to build a single span footbridge over the M A track, is a most unfortunate but necessary step in getting a safe crossing constructed for the mothers and those young animals that attend the Primary *High* School."

"The official policy and duty of the borough council under current House of Common Animal legislation, is that it must 'assure as far as is *animalistically* possible, that all young animals must at all times be able to travel in safety to and from their school' and, as Spiders International Limited hold all the known patents for the construction of single span footbridges and overhead walkways, then the borough council together with the Directors of Reynard's, Serpents, Stoats and Weasels Limited, have to be free to negotiate any form of sub-contract with Spiders International Limited that they feel is necessary in pursuit of that objective. I commend Sly-

Fox and his colleagues for their quick response to resolving what can only be described as an unfortunate interference to their plans for the construction of a safe crossing into the Primary High School for Young Animals."

Sly-Fox, in his official capacity as a borough councillor, followed up his statement published in the news media and invited Black Rat, QC, MHCA, to a press conference called by himself, that was held at the borough council offices, where he further informed all the newspaper reporters and other media organisation representatives present, of the situation relating to the proposed construction of a footbridge. (He had previously to this informative meeting sent a preview of his presentation vie the web to Ms Nosey Parrot at 'The News of the Weald' informing her of his intentions, so as to give her a scoop and keep her sweet for some future underhand deal he may need to publicise). Sly-Fox emphasised that there would now have to be a change in policy direction by the borough council, as a footbridge would need to be built at the extra expense of WE rate payers of Animal Country Parkland, in place of the abandoned underpass that was to have been a public access to the Primary *High* School.

This, Sly-Fox stressed, was an unfortunate policy change due entirely to the Coroner's court verdict, which itself was based on the toxic poisoning results shown by the post-mortem examination on the late Mr Wiggly Worm. Sly-Fox stated that due to these unfortunate circumstances, he had no other alternative but to advise Reynard's and Serpents Civil Engineering and Construction Company Limited, acting on behalf of Animal Country Parkland Borough Council, to negotiate a 'sub-contract' for the construction of a footbridge with the Directors of Spiders International Limited. Sly-Fox also reiterated that calling in Spiders International Limited for the planning and construction of a footbridge over the M A track was due in its entirety to and as a direct result of, the Coroner's court verdict on the 'accidental death' of Mr Wiggly Worm.

Sly-Fox then advised the media reporters present that he would be asking for an immediate full borough council meeting to be convened with all parties concerned, in order to thrash out with those parties, details as to the ways and means that a footbridge may be built within the budget originally set by the borough council that was for the cost of building a tunnel, as far as that was possible. But, he emphasised, that would depend to a great extent on the good will of the Directors of Spiders International Limited. Then, feeling he had past the onus of responsibility of building a footbridge onto Spiders International Limited, he gave one of his famously cunning Sly-Fox grins, closed the meeting and exited the room before any embarrassing questions could be put to him.

It was shortly after 'soft talking' to the media organisations that Sly-Fox put on his other hat as Chairman of the Bridge Club Committee and called an emergency meeting of its members at the Bridge Club's 19th Green Golf Club. When the committee had assembled, Sly-Fox opened the meeting in the Bridge Club's 'sound insulated boardroom' by explaining the dilemma they now found themselves in by having to go 'cap in hand' to Spiders International Limited to ask if it would accept a contract to construct a footbridge. For, as Sly-Fox explained, they all knew how volatile

Ms Black-Widow Spider's, (Managing Director of Spiders International Limited), mercurial temper could be and it would be even more so when she is asked if she would immediately release sets of plans from which the borough councillors may select a plan that they deem would be best suited for a footbridge crossing over the M A track. For it had to be a design based on a 'utility type patent', the cheapest possible version that Spiders International Limited made available on the open market, by means of their worldwide websites.

Sly-Fox asked the assembled Bridge Club Committee members if they had any ideas or questions they wished to air with the other club members. Venomous Viper, JP, hissed, "I've got a question. Why call in the spiders at all? Surely we could arrange to obtain a set of bridge construction plans from Spiders International's portfolio of patented plans and get our draftsmen to manipulate a modified redraft. After all, if a rose by any other name is still a rose – then a bridge by any other name must still be a bridge. What's more", Venomous Viper, JP, hissed, "we, (Reynard's, Serpents, Stoats and Weasels Limited), could not only build the M A track bridge but we could go into the bridge building business on our own account as bona-fide bridge building civil engineering contractors, in competition with the spiders."

Sly-Fox looked around the assembled Bridge Club members with half closed eyes before replying. Then he said,

"Let me put you in the picture before any more of you make a similar stupid remark like that. Spiders are not only the masters at constructing overhead websites and bridges they are also able to work at night, in the dark. This is no doubt because they have eight eyes. They all work and move about in absolute silence, quite possibly because they have eight legs too. They also have an in-built spinet and can cover large areas of any site of their own choosing with silken thread and what's more, they can spin the most complicated, complex and durable structures in a very short space of time. We would never be able to compete with them, even if we could obtain patents that would enable us to do it."

"But," said 'Slippery' Grass Snake, "will a footbridge, built by spiders, be strong enough to hold the weight of umpteen young, boisterous animals accompanied by their mothers?"

"Let me spell the facts out to all of you without any engineering experience,"' said Sly-Fox. "A single strand of spider's thread is strength for strength, stronger and far lighter than any known steel or other metals. It also comes with an added bonus; it's waterproof and rust proof. Because of this a spider's built footbridge will always be maintenance free. Another bonus is that there is no transportation or on site delivery costs as spiders always carry all their own equipment with them. That fact alone should minimise the overall cost of building a footbridge, with the added bonus that there will be no additional 'on site animal track transport'. Even now, animals get grid locked on the M A track twice a day - when cows have to pass over it to be milked and when faster traffic gets held up behind two of the larger dogs running side by side. Those factors alone cause further animal track congestion, with increased costs having to be levied onto the rate paying animals of Animal Country Parkland. It would be a very stupid political ploy on our part at this time to foist those extra costs onto the electorate, particularly as it's an election year, believe me."

Sly-Fox continued, "What's more, we shall not be forgiven too easily by the young animal's mothers that live in Animal Country Parkland for abandoning the tunnel under the animal track if a bridge isn't built as a substitute, especially as it was to have been a safe public access into the Primary *High* School. Don't forget, either, the bridge will be in *my* constituency and it is because of these arguments, not in spite of them, that I propose, no, I insist that we ask Spiders International Limited to undertake the building of a footbridge over the M A track junction. That's my proposal, OK?"

"I'll second that proposal," blurted out Councillor Dipper Magpie, JP.

"Then all of you in favour of the proposal say 'aye'," Sly-Fox ordered.

The 'aye's' came in a single vocal shout and the Bridge Club Committee members passed the motion as though it had been brought about by a large dose of mouth induced senna-pod extract or Epsom salts. That is, it came very quickly.

Sly-Fox then closed the meeting in his usual fashion and without so much as a 'goodnight', he made his way out of the golf club and hurried back to his lair in order to prepare for his forthcoming meeting with Ms Black-Widow Spider, the daunting and much feared Managing Director of Spiders International Limited.

PART 6

Sly-Fox consulted
Ms Black-Widow Spider

When Sly-Fox made an approach to Spiders International Limited through the international website, Ms Red Back Spider, the company's Australian website receptionist, politely asked him to wait a moment. She then informed him that Ms Black-Widow Spider, the Managing Director, was unavailable at that moment but she would put him through to her secretary, Ms Funnel-Web Spider, who promptly informed Sly-Fox that her boss had anticipated he would call owing to his announcement over the county website but she had left a message for him. The message was that she was unable to arrange a meeting with him at present as she had a full schedule but if he would care to arrange a meeting with her secretary, she would see him as soon as it was convenient.

Sly-Fox was outraged by this obvious slight. He wasn't used to being treated in such an offish manner. It was usually *he* who snubbed or kept other animals waiting but on this occasion he had to swallow his pride. Ms Black-Widow Spider held all the patents for bridge construction within the Spiders International Limited portfolio of bridge plans and she could strike a hard bargain if he pressed her too hard to sign a contract for building a suitable footbridge crossing over the notoriously dangerous M A track road junction.

However, on the following day Sly-Fox received a personal message from Ms Black-Widow Spider over the web, advising him he could come to her office at his earliest convenience with his colleagues to select the design for a footbridge and to arrange for her surveyor and engineers to study the site where the bridge was to be built and, if they could come to an amicable agreement, subsequently sign a contract. A working lunch would also be provided for him and his colleagues during the meeting.

Sly-Fox was elated. He agreed immediately over the web to a midday meeting, followed by luncheon with her and her team of experts and his councillor colleagues, their Planning and Construction Advisory Officers and representatives from Reynard's, Serpents, Stoats and Weasels Limited. The meeting was to be held in the boardroom at Spiders International Limited on the morrow and after coming off the web, he told his secretary to inform 'Slippery' Grass Snake, the borough council's Senior Executive Officer and his councillor colleagues who sat on the Planning and Construction Committee, together with the Managing Director of Reynard's, Serpents, Stoats and Weasels Limited, so as to be sure they attended the meeting and that they should be prepared to do some hard bargaining in securing a contractual obligation with Spiders International Limited.

Ms Black-Widow Spider, having arranged the meeting with Sly-Fox, quickly convened an emergency meeting with her fellow Directors to determine what their attitude was to building a footbridge over the animal track at the M A track intersection. She explained that in her opinion, if they could convince the borough councillors and Reynard's and Serpents company Directors to let them have a free hand in choosing the design structure of the proposed bridge, then they, the spiders, could build a web bridge at a reasonably low cost providing, she further explained, that such a bridge could be used as a night trap to catch unwary prey, therefore serving as a web-trap to provide a permanent food source for all the spiders living in that area. The spider Directors agreed unanimously to this proposition and gave their unbridled backing to Ms Black-Widow Spider as Managing Director, to agree a contract on these terms.

As arranged over the web network, at the appointed time on the following day, Sly-Fox and his council colleagues arrived at the offices of Spiders International Limited in an official borough council horse-drawn Landau, where Reynard's, Serpents, Stoats and Weasels company Directors were already seated in the boardroom, eating sandwiches and drinking what appeared to be glasses of white wine. Ms Black-Widow Spider was seated at the far end of the table, with all her four pairs of legs crossed, sipping what appeared to be a Bloody Mary from a small wine glass. Beside her sat Ms Funnel-Web Spider, her secretary, with a note pad and a pre-prepared contract ready to be signed.

When they were all seated round the table, Ms Black-Widow Spider introduced herself and asked Sly-Fox to introduce his council colleagues. Sly-Fox, with a flick of a paw in his colleague's direction said,

"For the borough council's Planning and Construction Projects Committee there is myself, Sly-Fox, Councillor Dipper Magpie, JP, Deputy Mayor, Councillor Venomous Viper, JP, and the council's Senior Executive Officer, Mr Grass Snake, who is accompanied by his secretary, Ms Pussy Cat, who will be taking notes."

"And for Reynard's, Serpents, Stoats and Weasels?" Ms Black-Widow Spider asked,

"I'm Punic Stoat and I lead the Reynard's team," replied Punic Stoat. "On my immediate right is the company secretary, Ms Ermine Mink, then Mr Cant Polecat and at the end of the table is Mr Willy Weasel."

"Well, well!" said Ms Black-Widow Spider, "if the evil one should cast his net but perhaps I'll cast mine instead, I will commence this meeting by stating categorically for the record, that we are here to discuss the construction of a footbridge crossing over the M A track with the objective of this exercise being to provide a safe access into the Primary *High* School for the young school pupils. My Directors have been made fully aware of the reasons for the footbridge and they are extremely sympathetic to the cause. I have therefore taken the liberty of producing three sets of patented plans from our company's portfolio any of which our company is prepared to construct at your earliest convenience, if you are amicable in accepting the terms and conditions we have drawn up in this contract." She then turned to her secretary, Ms Funnel-Web Spider and said,

"Distribute photocopies of the prepared plans and contracts to each of the representatives present, Ms Funnel-Web. But first I suggest each representative should look at the plans and then the contract before coming to a joint decision."

Sly-Fox said, "Once we have studied the plans and the terms of the contract, when would be a convenient time to negotiate a reply?"

"In thirty minutes time or the offer is off," said Ms Black-Widow Spider. "We have a very large order book with clients worldwide asking for websites, funnel webs and bridges. None of you can quibble at the 'barter price offer terms' we are to charge for this contract, on completion of course. Just choose a plan from the three on offer and I guarantee the bridge will be given a priority listing. I'll come back in twenty eight minutes for your decision; you have already wasted two minutes of your time." And without any more ado, she left the boardroom closely followed by Ms Funnel-Web Spider.

Twenty eight minutes had passed when, to the second, Ms Black-Widow Spider re-entered the boardroom with her secretary. The borough councillors and their officials and Reynard's and Serpents Directors were sitting bemused and docile at the boardroom table waiting for her return.

When Ms Black-Widow Spider and Ms Funnel-Web Spider had taken their seats at the head of the table, Sly-Fox rose up on his hind legs, leaned across the table towards her and in a perverse but conciliatory manner said,

"I'm speaking on behalf of Animal Country Parkland Borough Councillors and Reynard's and Serpents Directors, to say we accept the conditions contained in the 'barter contract'. In fact, we think the conditions laid down in the contract are fair and reasonable under the circumstances," said Sly-Fox.

"So I think you should," Ms Black-Widow Spider curtly replied. "After all, I do know how all of you operate your businesses."

They turned towards her in utter surprise and Sly-Fox asked, "How could you possibly know that?"

"Well, Well!" exclaimed Ms Black-Widow Spider, "there was I thinking you were all intelligent animals yet not one of you had worked out who it was that set up and operates the tabloid and 'web networks'. It's about time you learnt that there is nothing we spiders don't know about. We have reporters everywhere that send their reports to our Staff Editor at 'The News of the Weald', reports that are then sent on to me." Then, picking up one of the three sets of plans, she said, "I believe this is the footbridge you have chosen of the three on offer?" and smiling, turned and winked four of her eight eyes at Sly-Fox.

"Yes, well, that's the set of plans we have agreed on," replied Sly-Fox, "though we are of the opinion they are actually very similar, each of them has high sides, in fact, one can only describe them as being positively an inverted web shape."

"Yes, one could say that," said Ms Black-Widow Spider, "that's because we spiders have discovered over millions of years, 395 million years as a matter of fact, that webs are the strongest construction for anything permanently suspended in space. By the way, you do all understand that payment on completion of the contract must be immediate? I do mean immediate. Our accountants, Money Spiders Incorporated Limited, don't stand any shenanigans with late or none payers. Retribution for late or non-payment shall be immediate. I do mean immediate. Well, if that is all, I bid you all good day. My secretary will show you out. I will see the construction of the footbridge is given priority and you will receive a bill from us as soon as the footbridge crossing is completed."

"The borough council's accountant would prefer it if you would accept a cheque, Ms Black-Widow Spider," Sly–Fox said.

Ms Black-Widow Spider smiled, winked four of her eight eyes towards all of them and replied,

"I do suppose you would prefer to settle your debts that way but I would have thought male animals with your vast knowledge of the business world would have known the answer to that question. It's simply as I have just explained, that we spiders have our own banking system that's run by Money Spiders Incorporated Limited." Then she turned and walked out of the boardroom leaving her secretary, Ms Funnel-Web Spider to show them all out of the building. All of them that is, except Sly-Fox who, unbeknown to his councillor colleagues or the Directors of Reynard's and Serpents, slipped surreptitiously into Ms Black-Widow Spider's office and whispered to her,

"You obviously know there is to be local council elections shortly. Do you think your engineers could make a start on the footbridge before polling day?"

Ms Black-Widow Spider smiled, "I think we can do a deal on that issue, Sly-Fox. If you close your eyes to the semi-circular web structures we put in place to support either side of the footbridge, I'll see what I can do about getting priority given to the construction of the footbridge being built before the forthcoming elections."

"Sure. That's agreed then," Sly-Fox said, "I'm depending on you."

Ms Black-Widow Spider nodded her agreement and Sly-Fox walked quickly out of her office and with a supercilious, smug grin contorting his face, he followed his fellow councillor compatriots and crooked cronies of Reynard's and Serpents onto the cart-park, from where they got into their various modes of transport and drove away.

Part 7

A Miracle; the spinet spider's footbridge

It was late that same evening, as the tired, old sun finished its day's work, sinking below the skyline into the timelessness of space and a smiling new moon began its long, slow climb up into a cloudless night's sky to welcome the twinkling stars that were beginning to appear far out in space, when the screech of an owl was heard coming from the bell tower of the village church; an ancient Norman building half hidden from the country lane by Yew Trees growing in profusion over the graves located in the ancient church yard.

Church Lane had been the site chosen, supposedly by Animal Country Parkland Borough Council, for the installation of the new footbridge that was to cross over the M A track junction but in fact, it was Sly-Fox who had selected the site, which lay in close proximity to his golf club.

Pipistrelle bats were already flitting about the heavens like demented demons, sending out high pitched, sonic sounds that bounced off their prey allowing them to chase their victims as only bats can do, when an army of spinner spiders were seen by the wide-eyed barn owl marching silently towards the intersection where the A track merged with an intersection of the M A track, which was about to become the site of the footbridge that would lead into the Primary *High* School for Young Animals.

Wide-eyed with his beak agape, the old grey feathered owl watched with fascination as spiders shimmied up trees and swung across the M A track like the trapeze artists they are, to attach guide web-stays from one tree to another. At the same time, their workmates scaled up and down the thin, silken thread lines from support stays, spinning whole masses of threads into a single web that was then overlaid with fine, close knitted gossamer to form a walkway. Then, when the spiders had completed that work operation, they attached the ends of each side of the web to the overhead mainstays, which were then hoisted up into the treetops to create a magnificently arched footbridge.

Throughout the whole night, not a sound was heard as the spinner spiders worked to complete their assigned tasks and, before the new day had broken to waken cockerels to perform their duty of sounding *animal reveille,* the spinner spiders having completed the footbridge, got *fell in* and marched off in complete silence to wherever spiders disappear to during the daytime, thus leaving the magnificence of their work for all other animals to marvel at. The footbridge seemed to hang from the very heavens itself and on becoming covered in morning dew, it glistened in the rays of the rising sun; rays that lit each dewdrop as if it was a fairy light set on a twig in a woodland glade or dewdrops that had spread themselves over green meadow pastures in the countryside on early autumn mornings. The bridge, with its fairy lights, was indeed a magnificent sight to behold.

Sly-Fox was sitting in the office of Animal Country Parkland Borough Council's Senior Executive Officer when the morning mail arrived. The first letter 'Slippery' Grass Snake opened was the 'barter bill' from Ms Black-Widow Spider that read,

To:
Mr Grass Snake,
Senior Executive Officer,
C/o The Borough Council Offices,
Animal Country Parkland, ACP KC

Sir,

<u>For Your **Immediate**</u> Attention.

Spiders International Limited require *immediate payment in full* for construction of the new footbridge that is now in place at the M A / A track junction between Animal Country Woodlands at Church Lane and the Primary *High* School, as per the contractual arrangement made between Animal Country Parkland Borough Council, the recipient, and Reynard's and Serpents Civil Engineering Company Limited, the formal civil engineering contractor for the M A / A track footbridge project.

Yours truly,
Black Widow Spider for and on behalf of,
Spiders International Limited.

'Slippery' Grass Snake read the letter. His facial expression turned into a deep frown, he looked up at Sly-Fox and passed the letter to him. Sly-Fox read the letter and, jumping out of his chair, he dashed out of the office, down two flights of stairs and into the street, where he was almost knocked down by a Great Dane that was trundling along the High Street, and he didn't stop running till he came to the site of the new footbridge. He stood gawking at the beautiful structure in awe, unable to comprehend how spiders could have built such a wonderful bridge in a single night. It was a miracle. He stood dumbstruck and panting for breath where he was for several minutes before first 'Slippery' Grass Snake then Councillor Venomous Viper, JP, slithered up to him.

"By-Golly," hissed 'Slippery' Grass Snake.

"Good-Golly," hissed Councillor Venomous Viper, JP.

"Glory be to Golly," said Sly-Fox, "quickly, now get back to the council offices. We must get the council's accountants to send off a 'barter account settlement docket' to Money Spiders International Limited - post-haste."

"Let them wait for their 'barter docket' like everyone else has to," said 'Slippery' Grass Snake, the borough's Senior Executive Officer. "Our accountants work on a six monthly payment cycle. They won't take kindly to having their routine altered."

"He's right," said Councillor Venomous Viper, JP. "Let them wait. There's not much they can do about it except take us to the County Court. Judge Bluebottle is the Circuit Judge. The spiders won't get much sympathy from him. He hates spiders."

"Who doesn't?" said Sly-Fox, raising the level of his bark. "But what you fail to appreciate is that a spider is like the Sword of Damocles, it can hang down from the heavens on a single thread and if it should drop down, it's deadly. Don't you realise there are millions of spiders everywhere, listening in and watching from their websites. They're just waiting for an order from that pugnacious Ms Black-Widow Spider to strike at us if we fail to keep faith with her."

Then, with that dire warning to the two serpents not to even contemplate reneging on the terms and conditions of the contract they had agreed with Ms Black-Widow Spider, Sly-Fox having convinced them of the danger they would be placing themselves in if the contract were not complied with, trotted off leaving the two reptiles to slither their way back to the borough council's offices. Both now trembled like moulded jellies as they had to order the accounts officer to send a 'barter bill account settlement docket' immediately to Money Spiders International Limited, before Ms Black-Widow Spider could use their failure to pay up as a reason to wreak her volatile, pugnacious vengeance on all of them.

However, unbeknown to Sly-Fox, Grass Snake or Venomous Viper, JP, millions of spiders already had their hundreds of millions eight half-closed eyes menacingly focused on them through their websites, ready to strike should they receive an order from Ms Black-Widow Spider to do so. But the three supposedly socially upstanding pillars of Animal Country Parkland society, members of the 19th Green Bridge Club Committee, (the covert branch of a money laundering and civil engineering contract manipulating international cartel organisation; an organisation that employed *hit-animals* to permanently remove *shysters* and *defaulters* who failed to settle business payments or contract obligations on time, to the benefit of this worldwide criminally operated syndicate), made their way post-haste back to 'Slippery' Grass Snake's borough council office to arrange payment to Spiders International Limited via Money Spiders International Limited, before they themselves were 'put paid to'.

However, Sly-Fox knew from information picked up on his own website and from personal knowledge of his past experiences of former, *late missing contemporaries*, that he had finally managed to convince his two somewhat doubting compatriots of the dangers inherent with failing to fulfil the conditions of this particular 'barter contract' with Ms Black-Widow Spider and her associates at Spiders International Limited. For as he adamantly pointed out,

"There's no hiding place from spiders. They're like the Almighty Golly. They're omnipotent and omniscient - but unlike Golly - they have three extreme differences:

They're omnivorous, carnivorous and cannibalistic. What's more, spiders can pinpoint the very spot where any animal is, at any given time, anywhere on earth through their international website networks.

"Do you understand?" He put one front paw up to his lip and with his other front paw he pointed at a cobweb hanging from the ceiling. He hissed, "Shush, webs *are* ears."

When the three arrived back at the council offices they immediately set the borough accountant to work, forwarding a 'barter bill of exchange docket' direct to Money Spiders International Limited by the Express Carrier Pigeon Messenger Service. Sly-Fox then dictated a note to 'Slippery' Grass Snake's secretary, Ms Pussy Cat and ordered her to send a copy direct to each member of the 19th Green Bridge Club Committee, informing them that,

'An emergency meeting (with a working breakfast) will be held in The Bridge Club Committee boardroom tomorrow at 9.30 am sharp, stop. Urgent. No defaulters, stop. This is an order not a request, stop. S-F.'

After seeing that copies of his message had been addressed to each member of the Bridge Club Committee and were sent out separately, Sly-Fox then had Ms Pussy Cat forward a note to the golf club's resident steward, Mr House Mouse. It was a message advising Mr House Mouse of the arrangements Sly-Fox had made for the following day. Sly-Fox also ordered Mr House Mouse to purchase poison; the most pungent spider killing agent he could lay his tiny paws on. He then added a PS, which read,

'*Under no circumstances are you to use a website to communicate with me, stop. If you should for any reason have to contact me, only do so by Express Carrier Pigeon Messenger Service, stop. S-F.*'

Sly-Fox then sent two further letters by the Express Carrier Pigeon Messenger Service, one to each of the Bridge Club Committee's henchmen, the American, Fetid Skunk and the Canadian, Vicious Mink. The messages read,

'Attend 19th Green clubhouse at 08.00 am tomorrow morning, stop. Clubhouse steward will provide you with insecticide, stop. Fumigate the whole area beneath Bridge Club boardroom, stop. See that *all* spiders' webs and loose gossamer are removed from beneath and within the boardroom before the Bridge Club Committee goes into session tomorrow morning at 09.30 am, stop. Do not under any circumstances mention anything about this message over any website, stop. If you have any doubts about the content of this message, communicate with me only by Express Carrier Pigeon Messenger Service, stop. My life and your lives may depend on your vigilance and diligence, stop. This message is to be treated as Top Secret and urgent, stop. Destroy this message once read, stop. S-F.'

Before 9.30 am the following morning, all of the Bridge Club Committee members were seated round the boardroom mahogany table. Each one of them was tucking into their chosen breakfast, which was 'self-served' from a row of hotplates and a large Bain Marie, all of which were arranged on a specially built sideboard; a piece of furniture that was also designed to insulate the boardroom wall from any possible eaves dropping devices that may be used to obtain intelligence from within that enclave, by other animals seeking to gain evidence as to the real functions and intentions of the devious and cunning conspirators locked away behind heavy wooden mahogany, steel plated, sound proofed doors.

When Sly-Fox arrived at the 19th Green, the golf club appeared to all intents and purposes to be battened and barred but there was a side entrance, which led into the foyer of the club for which only two animals held a key. The club steward, Mr House Mouse, held one; Sly-Fox held the other key himself. After entering the clubhouse through the side door, Sly-Fox made his way to the Bridge Club boardroom, where he quickly helped himself to some of the breakfast items on offer and poured himself a cup of strong coffee. He then sat down at the head of the boardroom table and called the meeting to order. Ms Ermine Stoat, the Bridge Club Committee's secretary, took out her shorthand note pad and wrote a list of all those present. For security reasons, each member had a number in place of his name but names were used between members at Bridge Club Committee meetings. The members present at this meeting were:

Chairman Sly-Fox; Deputy Chairman Venomous Viper, JP; Members Messrs Foxy-Fox, Dipper Magpie, JP, 'Slippery' Grass Snake, Punic Stoat, Cant Polecat, Willy Weasel and senior police Superintendent Sniffer Blood Hound. Representing their business partners from America was Mr Fetid Skunk and from Canada Mr Vicious Mink.

Sly-Fox opened the meeting by asking Fetid Skunk and Vicious Mink,

"Is the deed done?" referring to the removal of all the resident spiders by lethal insecticide and the removal of their cobwebs and gossamer from beneath the Bridge Club Committee's boardroom. The two assassins nodded to acknowledge that the terrible deed had been carried out. Then Sly-Fox began by stating the obvious and said,

"To those of you who may as yet be unaware, a footbridge over the M A / A track junction has been erected in record time by Spiders International Limited. It has been an incredible achievement, in so far as all the work on the footbridge has been carried out in a single night, in the dark and in absolute silence. It is an uncanny, brilliant civil engineering achievement by those widely despised animals, spiders. But now, as all of you present will be aware, there is the local election to be held in the very near future and, as Spiders International Limited have built the footbridge over the M A / A track junction that leads to the Primary *High* School, I suggest,' said Sly-Fox putting on one of his famous foxy smiles, "that when the young animals are away from school on their summer holidays, this would be an opportune time to arrange a civic opening for the footbridge, so as to gain maximum publicity for our party's candidates in the local election, while at the same time enhancing Black Rat's chances of re-election as our MHCA at the next General Election." Sly-Fox then asked the assembled miscreants,

"What suggestions do any of you have?"

The committee members sat for some time cogitating, some scratching their fur, others furrowing their brows, till Ms Ermine Stoat tentatively raised her right paw.

"Do you have a suggestion, Ms Ermine?"

"Yes, Sir, or at least I think I have," she replied.

"Then what do you suggest we might do, my dear?" said Sly-Fox.

"Well, Sir," she replied, "it seems to me that we need to get national as well as local media coverage for the school footbridge opening. This footbridge is unique in so far as it is the first suspension bridge ever to be built over an M A / A track specifically for the benefit of young animals to get safely to and from school. Now, it's my opinion that if we are to attract the maximum publicity for the footbridge opening, we should approach His Royal Highness (HRH) Prince Porpoise, the Prince of Whales, to see if he would consent to opening the bridge."

"And what do you suggest we say to HRH that may persuade him to come to Animal Country Parkland to open our bridge?" enquired Dipper Magpie, JP.

"Well, it could be to explain to His Royal Highness how unique the footbridge is and that his presence and opening the bridge would be seen as a stamp of approval for its design, structure and cosmetic beauty. We could further explain that His Royal presence at the opening of the footbridge would also enhance opportunities for the construction of similar bridges over other dangerous roads and river crossings. And also, that it will enhance our chances of producing similar structures for the export market. I'm sure HRH is fully aware how vital export markets are to our nation's interest."

"But my dear Ms Ermine," said Sly-Fox. 'The footbridge is patented. The patent is the property of Spiders International Limited and the spiders guard their patent rights jealously."

"Yes, Sir, I am aware of that but I was careful not to suggest Reynard's, Serpents and Stoats would build such bridges abroad. I only mentioned it may enhance the opportunity for exporting similar structures. What the Prince's advisers make of that statement is one thing, the reality of the fact is entirely another."

"Got you," hissed Venomous Viper, JP.

"A brilliant idea," chirped Dipper Magpie, JP.

Sly-Fox smiled as he grasped the significance of such a proposal before asking Ms Ermine, "Have you anything to add to that suggestion?"

"Yes, there is another reason why the Prince may wish to attend the footbridge opening."

"And that is?" questioned Sly-Fox.

"The Prince has had a bad press lately due to his widely reported 'extra marital' philandering. If we get our timing right and 'suck up' to the media on His Royal Highnesses behalf, we can inform the press and television that they will be given every facility they require in order to get photographic coverage of HRH and the event. This ruse will surely increase the Prince's reputation with the general public after the event, especially among the young and female animals of the borough."

"Well, well,"' said Sly-Fox, "I'm bemused by the logic of your reasoning my dear. Are we all agreed on Ms Ermine's marvellously contrived suggestion?"

There was silence for several seconds while the conspirators inwardly digested Ms Ermine Stoat's political prognosis of her ideas then a concerted agreement began with a 'nod-nod' here, an 'aye-aye' there and 'here-here' there, resounding from all round the boardroom table.

"Right, now I think that's a job for the borough council's Press Release Officer. We'll leave that for you to deal with 'Slippery'," said Sly-Fox winking at the council's Senior Executive Officer. Then Sly-Fox barked, "Oh! I almost forgot, 'Slippery' don't forget to arrange a press conference. I think as Chairman of the Planning and Construction Committee, it should be I who presides over any media presentation, that's of course if we get confirmation of a Royal Visit to our borough."

"Isn't there something else you may have forgotten, Sly-Fox?" chirped up Dipper Magpie JP.

"And what may that be?" Sly-Fox barked angrily.

"Policing the event, of course, what shall we do about policing?"

"That's not a problem," bayed Superintendent Blood Hound, "I'll have the borough under police hound supervision with diversionary traffic signs put in place. I'll have fire armed surveillance teams standing by on the rooftops in every nook and cranny. They will cover the whole of the Royal route for the whole period of HRH's visit. It'll cost the rate payers a bit in extra police overtime but who cares about that?"

"Well, that's settled then you old dog. We'll leave that job in your capable paws." Then Sly-Fox suddenly said, "Do not forget, the local elections are soon. You all know that time is running short till Election Day. We need to get the business of this Royal Visit sorted out soon or we'll have to make alternative arrangements for opening the bridge - get a film star such as Rin-Tin-Tin, Bambi, Lassie or whoever is in the lime-light of the animal film star world. Right, now that concludes our business for the moment." Then, in his usual rude manner, Sly-Fox got up from the table, quickly trotted off out of the room and left them to work out their own devices.

Mr Grass Snake hurriedly finished eating his *working breakfast* and quickly made his way to his council office, where he promptly set his junior council colleagues to work on preparing a documentary request to the Royal Palace, asking in the most subservient terms *they* could dream up, if Prince Porpoise, The Prince of Whales, would condescend to open the newly constructed, ultra-modern, designed footbridge sited in the borough of

Animal Country Parkland in the county of Cantium. Grass Snake himself then outlined what he thought should be arranged within the Royal schedule. This included the Prince's arrival but far more importantly, in his opinion, the precedence of presentation. He therefore included in *his* letter of request to the Royal Palace that,

'Should your Royal Highness consent to attend and open the borough's newly constructed footbridge, a facility, Your Royal Highness, that is in fact the first such crossing of its kind ever to be designed and constructed by any borough council within the whole of the animal kingdom and specifically for young animals to safely attend the borough councils Primary *High* School. The footbridge is a unique facility that has been specially designed and constructed by Animal Country Parkland Borough Council, to be a safe crossing over an ultra busy animal M A / A track junction, for the benefit of young animals and their mothers residing in the borough of Animal Country Parkland.

Furthermore your Highness, with this in mind, may I humbly suggest that Your Royal Highness accepts that the opening of the footbridge should take place on the same day that the young animals return to school, which is in six weeks time, if that can be arranged within your schedule? Then, when Your Royal Highness cuts the ribbon and walks across the footbridge, that the young animals shall follow Your Royal Highness in a similar manner to that of the children in Robert Browning's poem 'The Pied Piper of Hamlin Town'. A fiddler shall be employed for this purpose should Your Royal Highness agree to this suggestion. His Worship the Mayor and the Civic Corporation are sure Your Royal Highness will simply enjoy such a unique experience, should Your Royal Highness care to accept the borough council's loyal invitation?'

'This invitation, Your Royal Highness, is dispatched on behalf of His Worship the Mayor, Councillor Gobbler Turkey; Sly-Fox, Chairman of the borough council's Planning and Construction Committee and, the borough councillors representing Her Majesty's loyal subjects of Animal Country Parkland.'

'Signed on behalf of the borough of Animal Country Parkland.'

'Grass Snake (Mr),'

'Senior Executive Officer,'

PART 8

Ms Black-Widow Spider exclaimed, "What has happened to my website transmissions?"

It was 11.00 am precisely when Ms Black-Widow Spider asked Ms Red Back Spider, her website transmission operator, to put her through to the resident spiders that lived beneath the Bridge Club boardroom. Ms Black-Widow Spider was intent on obtaining information as to what had transpired at that morning's Bridge Club Committee meeting, especially if it concerned or bore any relationship to the footbridge package deal that Spiders International Limited had undertaken for Animal Country Parkland Borough Council. However, the spider service engineers told Ms Red back Spider his website engineers were having trouble connecting transmission signals with the web network installed in all areas of and near to the Bridge Club Committee boardroom. Ms Red Back Spider went immediately into Ms Black-Widow Spider's office and explained to her that all communications with the residence in and under the 19th Green Bridge Club Committee rooms were dysfunctional. So, using her private website,

Ms Black-Widow Spider contacted the spider's senior website Service Communications Engineer and demanded to know,

"What has happened to my website transmissions to the 19th Green boardroom offices at the golf club?"

"I've no idea," the senior website Communications Service Engineer told her. "This situation is unprecedented throughout the whole of our spider website history. My web strand engineers are out now trying to track the fault. I can't understand it. It's never, ever happened before. My web repair linesmen are doing their best to find and remedy the fault. What else do you expect them to do about it?"

"Do about it? Get it sorted out pronto, that's what I want you to do!"

"Then I'll need you to sanction that order in writing. Send me a 'search and find docket' and I'll send another website repair crew out there right away."

"A 'search and find docket' is on its way. Now get moving. There's something not quite right here. This is obviously one of Sly-Fox's evil doings, which means it's a serious matter whatever he's up to."

"OK," replied the senior Communications Service Engineer, "I'll send my express team of daddy-long-legs to the job. They should arrive at the 19th Green clubhouse and the Bridge Club Committee rooms within the hour."

"That's good! Let me know immediately what the problem is as soon as your line engineers communicate with you and I do mean immediately."

"Right madam," he replied. Then getting onto his internal web line he vibrated into it in secret spider code,

"Daddy-long-legs proceed immediately to 19th Green clubhouse. Find whatever it is that's causing the break in our website communications system, reconnect the web threads and report back to me what it is that's caused the break in vibration communications on the website network. Get moving!"

A daddy-long-legs team of web thread repairers rushed off as fast as their long legs would carry them. When they arrived at the golf club it was closed up - battened and barred - and although they banged on the door and rang the bell, there was no reply.

"What are we going to do now?" said Charlie the chargehand daddy-long-legs. "We can't break-in without a Justice's warrant and a police hound in attendance." "No," replied Danny Short Legs, the daddy-long-legs website apprentice, "but I know a spider who can get in without actually breaking in." Then, without any more ado, he dashed over to the nearest pond and came back with a water spider. "This is my itinerant friend," said Danny Short Legs, "his name is Walter-Skater Spider and he can get into the main clubhouse building by walking along the top of the stream and climbing up beneath the boardroom floorboards. He's sure to discover something as most of our cousins who reside at the golf club live under the boardroom floor on their websites."

"Yes, that's a good idea and worth a try," Charlie the chargehand agreed. Then he told Walter-Skater Spider, "What we want to know is why we're not receiving any messages on our central website communications network from the 19th Green clubhouse and the Bridge Club Committee room. Right, you know what to look for, off you go and report back here as quickly as you possibly can."

Walter-Skater Spider hopped onto the surface of the stream and quickly disappeared from sight under the golf club, only to return almost as quickly with tears running from all eight of his large, all-seeing eyes. He reported to Charlie the chargehand that all the spiders that had lived under the Bridge Club Committee room were dead. Some of them were lying on the banks of the stream under the clubhouse; those that had fallen in the water had been washed away and not one of them had been left alive. "What's more," he said, "all the websites and gossamer have been ripped down and burned."

"Right, you've done a good job Walter-Skater Spider. Now cut out that silly boo-hooing," said Charlie the chargehand web thread engineer. "Now go back to your pond, get on your web and send this message to my senior website service engineer, and he wrote on a note pad,

'Sir, all of our cousins that lived in and under the clubhouse are dead, most possibly by poison, stop. All websites have been demolished and gossamer burnt, stop. I am about to enter the area below the Bridge Club Committee's boardroom to assess the damage and begin repairing the website network, stop. I should be through to you on the web within an hour, stop. Message ends, stop.'

Charlie, the chargehand daddy-long-legs gave the note to Walter-Skater Spider and told him,

"I can't emphasise to you just how important this message is. Now off you go and send it immediately when you get back to your website." Walter-Skater Spider ran off across the 17th and 18th greens to where his pond was to be found, hopped down the bank onto the surface of the water and skated to where his web was stretched between tall pond reeds. He then shimmied up into the centre of his web and sent the message as he had been instructed and waited till he received the reply, "Message received. Roger and out."

As soon as the senior website Service Communications Engineer had received the report from Charlie the chargehand daddy-long-legs, he immediately contacted Ms Red Back Spider, website operator to Ms Black-Widow Spider, Managing Director of Spiders International Limited.

"You're wanted on the web urgently, Madam," she said. "It's the senior website Service Communications Engineer. He won't tell me what it is, other than it's serious," and she walked out of the office leaving the door open for Ms Black-Widow Spider to follow her back into her office where the international communications master website was installed.

"Right," said Ms Black-Widow Spider, "have you found out why I was cut off from our spider websites at the 19th Green golf club Bridge Club Committee room?"

"Yes, I have," replied the senior Communications Engineer. "The answer to your question is simply that all our cousins that resided in and under the Bridge Club Committee's boardroom are dead. It looks as if they were poisoned with some form of highly lethal insecticide. My daddy-long-legs linesmen have managed to locate the golf club's resident steward, a Mr House Mouse. Mr House Mouse volunteered information that he had been ordered by Sly-Fox to purchase insecticide and that Sly-Fox had given him specific orders to be sure it was highly lethal, particularly to spiders."

"Was it the House Mouse that exterminated our cousins or were other animals involved?"

"House Mouse said he was told to leave the side door into the 19th Green clubhouse open this morning. There are only two keys to the side door entrance. He has one and Sly-Fox holds the other. He said Sly-Fox had told him to lock himself in his lodgings and to keep his curtains drawn closed but at 08.00 am he peeked out of his window. He told us he had seen Fetid Skunk, the American, together with Vic the Mink, his Canadian associate, come into the golf club via the side door he had left open. He'd heard them go into his store cupboard. He didn't know if they'd removed the insecticide, he could only guess they had, because Fetid Skunk took something into the Bridge Club Committee's boardroom and locked the door. Vic the Mink went out of the clubhouse through the side door and House Mouse heard him splashing about among the rocks in the stream below the Bridge Club Committee's boardroom. He said he had no idea what happened after that but both animals had attended the 09.30 am meeting of the Bridge Club Committee."

"You say he *had* no idea what happened after that, using *had* in the past tense?"

"Yes! Well, because he then apparently tried to run away from my daddy-long-legs but he got himself tangled up on one of our webs and unfortunately hanged himself on the threads, the poor thing."

"By Golly," said Ms Black-Widow Spider, "that was rather silly of Mr House Mouse wasn't it, especially as he was the only witness at the scene?"

"Yes, it was a most unfortunate accident and inconvenient too," the senior website Communications Service Engineer agreed. "But at least our daddy-long-legs managed to suck all the relevant information out of him before he died. And as Charlie, my daddy-long-legs chargehand told me, which I now repeat to you verbatim, "Anything can happen on a web.""

"Is there any other evidence as to what those rapscallions were doing other than massacring our cousins and destroying our website? What possible reason can they have for committing mass murder? What is that devious, cunning Bridge Club Committee up to now? What is so secret they are prepared to go to any lengths to achieve it? Of course, you can't answer those questions but at the very least we have found out who actually purchased the poison and we also know the identity of those killers who used it. We know too who gave the orders to those involved in the exterminations, don't we? Now you had better put me through on the web to Spiders Security Services," she ordered.

The website Communications Service Engineer connected the website threads to the website security office of Spiders International Website Security Services Limited. She was taken utterly by surprise when a bark from the other end of the web asked her,

"Can I help you? Canis-Hound here, acting senior security officer."

"Oh!" Ms Black-Widow Spider said in utter surprise, "I wish to speak with Tarantula-Spider?"

"Who's that asking?"

"Black-Widow Spider, Managing Director of Spiders International Limited."

"Oh! I thought you would have been informed Senior Tarantula-Spider has taken a spot of well earned leave, madam. He told me he intends to spend a bit of time on the golf course playing against his old friends in the police force, which includes me too. He mentioned especially wanting to play against senior police Superintendent Sniffer Blood Hound, who served under him in the county police service before Tarantula-Spider retired. I've taken over from Tarantula-Spider acting as senior security officer for Spiders International Website Security Services Limited as from this morning. Perhaps I should introduce myself; I'm former police Superintendent Canis-Hound. I served with Cantium Animal Countryside County police force for twenty five years. I'm surprised you've never heard of me?"

"No. Well, I don't play golf myself and I'm not directly responsible for security recruitment," said Ms Black-Widow Spider. "What's more, I wouldn't know one end of a golf club from the other but I do know senior Superintendent Sniffer Blood Hound. I've seen him quite often in the 19th Green clubhouse. He is reputed to be, by his colleagues, a very efficient police hound. He is highly respected and an upstanding pillar of local society and a revered member of the Bridge Club Committee. *So I'm led to understand."*

"Yes, so *am I*, a golf club member that is. Now, how can I help you madam?"

"You can't," replied Ms Black-Widow Spider, "I need to speak to Tarantula- Spider personally. I've got his home website number. I'll contact him there." She hung up, trembling with rage.

"By Golly," said Ms Black-Widow Spider to Ms Funnel-Web Spider after she came off the web, "I'm sure that Bridge Club Committee has taken over Spiders International Website Security Services. They will already know I've been informed over the web about the murders at the golf club. That new acting senior security officer, Canis-Hound, was on Cantium Animal Countryside County police force. He is also a member of the 19th Green golf club. You can bet he's already told his old senior, Sniffer Blood-Hound, that a new website has been installed at the golf club, damn him. I've got to contact Tarantula-Spider to find out why he has taken leave without informing me about it. There's something very sinister going on and we have got to find out just what that lot at the 19th Green of the golf club's Bridge Club Committee are really up to, especially as no unsavoury news has been published by 'The News of the Weald'. Get Tarantula-Spider on my internal website. He must know what they're setting up between them."

Tarantula-Spider was sitting in his garden, meditating over recent events that had progressed at lightning speed, which left him bewildered as to what was going on at Spiders International Limited. He had arrived at his office this very morning to find he had been given 'garden leave' and been replaced by Canis-Hound who had been a police Superintendent working under him when he was Cantium County Police Chief. His thoughts were then broken when his website began to give off Morse signal vibrations. He quickly jumped up and returned a simple message that read,

'Quit message. Call on me.'

Ms Black-Widow Spider turned to her secretary, who she had just called into her office and said,

"I think Tarantula-Spider may know what's going on. Order my chauffeur to fetch my buggy round to the rear door. I've got to go over to Tarantula-Spider's home to see him. He won't answer his web." She swept out of her office and headed straight for the rear door of the building, walking as fast as her eight legs would carry her, to wait for her chauffeur.

Ms Black-Widow Spider's chauffeur was none other than Lasiodora Klug, a heavyweight spider from Brazil. Klug was a huge brute of a spider that was devoted to his mistress. No sensible animal would ever want to physically tangle with him.

As soon as Klug had received the message to bring a buggy round to the rear door of Ms Black-Widow Spider's office, he knew something unusual was going on. He instantly harnessed up a Shetland pony to her personal buggy and trotted it round to where she was already waiting for him.

"Senior Tarantula's place, Klug," she said, "and don't do anything that can get us stopped by a police hound."

"Is there a problem Ms?" Klug asked.

"There could be," replied Ms Black-Widow Spider, "but if we are stopped by a police hound, would you deal with the problem in the usual way?"

"I'd be delighted to Ms," he said.

They passed along an animal track that led away from the office then turned onto an M A track for several miles, before turning off down a side lane that led into a coppice where Tarantula-Spider lived alone in his large detached abode. Tarantula-Spider was in his garden waiting by the front gate for Ms Black-Widow Spider to arrive. When she alighted from the buggy, Lasiodora Klug stood beside her. He first cast his eight eyes over Tarantula-Spider then he glanced about the coppice.

"It's quite safe here, at least for the present," Tarantula-Spider said, taking note of Klug's suspicion as to some possible danger. "There are no strangers about here at the moment. I have been on to the spinner spider's website and instructed them to warn me if any animals should come into my neighbourhood."

"Yes!" exclaimed Ms Black-Widow Spider, "that's what I've come to see you about, the websites. I think our international websites have been infiltrated by Reynard's and Serpents. That organisation is up to something. Did you know they have murdered all our cousins at the 19th Green clubhouse and all of those that lived under the Bridge Club Committee's boardroom too? They will no doubt know by now that you have invited me to come here and that you have asked to be warned about the approach of any strange animals."

"Yes, you are right. But by having that bit of information they won't dare show their faces around here - far too many witnesses, do you see?"

"Well, yes, I hadn't thought of that. Very clever of you, Tarantula," said Ms Black-Widow Spider. "Now for the reason I've come to see you."

"Oh, I do know why you've come," said Tarantula. "It's not only because the websites have been taken over but also to find out why I was given a spot of leave from Spiders International Website Security Services Limited without you having been informed. Am I right?"

"Yes, of course," replied Ms Black-Widow Spider. "But why were you?"

"I've no idea, really," said Tarantula-Spider, 'and if I had, I couldn't tell you because as I was leaving my office I was called back and *made* to sign the Animal Security Act. Although, for what reason I have absolutely no idea - except that my engineers did report to me earlier in the day that 'Slippery' Grass Snake, the Animal Country Parkland Borough Council's Senior Executive Officer, has sent a message to the Royal Palace inviting Prince Porpoise, The Prince of Whales, to come to Parkland and open the new footbridge over the M A / A track junction. Yes, that's what this is all about, Royal Protection. That Canis-Hound who has taken over my job on a 'temporary basis' is attached to the Royal Protection Group (RPG). It's the RPG that has taken over security arrangements for the Royal Visit."

"Ah!" exclaimed Ms Black-Widow Spider, "so RASCELS are not in control of our international websites. So what are they really up to?"

"It's got to be something they need to get control of, something really important to them locally, otherwise why murder our cousins under the Bridge Club boardroom?" said Tarantula.

"Yes and why should they ask Prince Porpoise to open *my bridge* without inviting me and my Directors of Spiders International Limited, unless they want to grab all the kudos, honours and publicity for themselves?" said Ms Black-Widow Spider.

"That's it! They want to get the media coverage that's what they're after. It's the local elections soon. Political power is their objective. Why, those devious, cunning, murderous, unmitigated rogues," Tarantula-Spider blurted out.

"Yes, I'm sure you're right Tarantula but because the footbridge is a supposedly all-council show with Sly-Fox being given the credit for its design and construction, we spiders have been left out of the limelight while that crafty Sly-Fox and his fellow conspirators get all the media coverage and all the glory for *our bridge*. I'll make him sorry for this, that devious, political, conniving, conspiring pervert and those cronies of his too, who were responsible for the assassination of our cousins. By Golly I shall," said a very irate Ms Black-Widow Spider.

"Of course, you're right but you've got to be very subtle in the way you go about dealing with those perverted, politically motivated megalomaniacs," said Tarantula-Spider. "Remember, the police are aware of the killings that took place at the 19th Green clubhouse and who was responsible for them by the messages that were sent over the website network. They may even be wondering why those deaths have not been reported to the Animal County Countryside police service. The Royal Protection Group may not be aware of senior Superintendent Sniffer Blood Hound's involvement with the Bridge Club Committee but even if they are, for security reasons they may stay their hand till after this Royal Visit is over before they go over the senior Superintendent's head and inform Wolf Hound, the county's Senior Constable, of the murders at the 19th Green golf club's Bridge Club Committee room."

"Don't worry, I'll have dealt with those miscreants myself by then, you can be sure of it, but I'll wait till the Royal Visit is over and the road to my revenge is not blocked by the terms of any formal protocol," said Ms Black-Widow Spider. Then she said,

"I blame myself for all this. The killing of our cousins at that damnable golf club is because I let on to Sly-Fox when I had secured the contract to build the M A / A track footbridge, that we spiders have access to all website information. That, my dear friend Tarantula, is the reason why Sly-Fox had his henchmen wipe out our operators at the communications centre under the Bridge Club Committee's boardroom." Ms Black-Widow Spider then shook her head, blinked her eight eyes and began to tap her eight feet before saying, "The sheer arrogance and cunning of that animal, it beggars belief. He's got to be taught a lesson, a final lesson that he won't live long enough to regret, so help me by Golly!"

"Of course you're right, my dear," replied Tarantula-Spider, "and perhaps a fitting end to Sly-Fox and his henchmen who had the temerity to kill our cousins and destroy our website, should be that they should die on a website."

"Mm, yes," said Ms Black-Widow Spider. "He that killed because of the web – then so shall he die on a web. He certainly shall when I wrap this case up."

PART 9

Ms Black-Widow Spider's
first inclination; to make a quick
and final example of Sly-Fox

Having discovered to her great relief that Spiders International Website had not been taken over by RASCELS, (in other words, Sly-Fox and his cronies of the 19th Green golf club's notorious Bridge Club Committee), but by the Royal Protection Group, Ms Black-Widow Spider began to hatch her plans for the punishment that was to be inflicted on the perpetrators of the deaths of her cousins and too the destruction of the spider's website beneath the Bridge Club Committee's boardroom.

Her first inclination was to make a quick example of Sly-Fox, the perpetrator and his two henchmen, Fetid Skunk and Vic the Mink, who had been responsible for carrying out the mass extermination of her cousins. Although her natural instinct was for taking such a rash course of impulsive action, she declined to follow it. What then should she do? After all, their punishments had to fit their crimes; it had to be slow, painful and permanent. What was more important, it had to be a dire warning to other would be criminals and assassins but for the moment, retributive punishment would have to wait till after the Royal Visit was over and things had returned to reasonable normality in the borough of Animal Country Parkland, Cantium.

The Royal Visit by Prince Porpoise, The Prince of Whales, had been an outstanding success. The arrangements made for the Royal Visit had been presided over by Sly-Fox but although they were the original brain child of Ms Ermine Mink, who put forward the ideas when the Bridge Club Committee had met to discuss the opening of the footbridge over the M A / A track junction, her ideas had been hyped up by 'Slippery' Grass Snake to be made to look as though they were of both his and Sly-Fox's inspiration. Therefore, Ms Ermine Mink's name was never mentioned, in any context, in the publicised plans for the Royal Visit.

When His Royal Highness had arrived in the borough of Animal Country Parkland on the day the new footbridge was to be opened, the Mayor and Aldermen of the borough were lined up to greet the Prince on his arrival at the Town Hall. His Worship, Councillor Gobbler Turkey, introduced His Royal Highness in turn to those animals that were deemed to be of a high social or political standing within the Parkland Borough Council's boundary. (Incidentally, all of those animals that were to be presented to the Royal Personage were either carnivores or carrion eaters; parasitic animals that thrived in their prosperity and influence only by living off the toil, sweat, blood and flesh of the living or dead of other more timid species of animals that lived in permanent fear of them in Animal Country Parkland).

There was, however, an anomaly in the presentation line-up. Ms Black-Widow Spider had not received an invitation to the opening of the footbridge, a spider designed and constructed footbridge. She was furious.

When the Prince's carriage arrived at the Town Hall, escorted by a bodyguard of swordfish outriders, the Mayor and Mayoress, Gobbler and Mrs Turkey, began the civic presentations. The first to be presented to His Royal Highness was Black Rat Q.C., MHCA for the constituency of Animal Country Parkland.. Gobbler Turkey began,

"Your Highness, this is Black Rat,QC,MHCA", He has given his uttermost support to the new footbridge project for the benefit of the young scholars of Animal Country Parkland," then he continued, "and this is *our very own* Councillor Sly-Fox. Sly-Fox is Chairman of Your Royal Highnesses visit Planning Committee. He is also Chairman of the borough council's Planning and Construction

Committee. He has held special responsibility for the planning and construction of the new footbridge that Your Highness is soon to open." He then continued tersely with the other presentations, "Mrs Sly-Fox, Councillor Venomous Viper, JP, Councillor Sly-Foxes right hand snake and Mrs Venomous Viper, JP; Councillor Dipper Magpie JP and Mrs Dipper Magpie; senior Superintendent Sniffer Blood Hound of Animal Country Parkland police force and Mrs Sniffer Blood Hound; Mr Grass Snake, the borough's Senior Executive Officer and Mrs Grass Snake." Gobbler Turkey then turned to present a second line of animals to be introduced and continued, "Here we have Your Highness, the Directors of the borough's major contractor, who have been engaged in the planning and construction of the new footbridge project, Mr Foxy-Fox, Chairman of RASCELS; Venomous Viper, JP Junior; Mr Willy Weasel, Mr Stoat and Mr Polecat," said Gobbler Turkey as His Royal Highness shook hands with the last of those animals to be presented before the footbridge was opened.

On having completed the formal introductions, the Mayor invited Prince Porpoise to take some light refreshments that had been prepared in the foyer of the council offices by the council's catering staff. Ms Snappy Yappy, (the overbearing Animal Country Parkland Borough Council's Yorkshire Terrier who was employed by the council as a front desk receptionist clerk but who was now acting as a temp-waitress), after giving a well rehearsed curtsy, sweetly 'yapp-yapped' as she asked the Prince, "What would be *Your Royal Highness's* pleasure?"

"His Royal Highness's pleasure," he told her, "is to be a cup of salt water (no sugar or milk) and a crab and seaweed sandwich (no salt)." Then after having rested for a short period away from those connivers, (mainly to get over the boredom of having to mix with such obnoxious, low bred, cunning animals than from the fatigue and physical exertion imposed on him by his visit), the Prince was advised by His Worship the Mayor, who had been told by Sly-Fox, who had himself been advised by Grass Snake, that it was time to make their way towards the footbridge so as to be ready for the official opening ceremony. It was an event that was to be broadcast throughout the Spiders International website networks. They were met as they left the council offices by a number of animals that were objecting to the new footbridge. As the Prince was leaving, there were a dozen or so snakes, stoats, polecats and weasels outside the council offices holding placards, waving banners, screaming and shouting in unison,

"We want a tunnel. We don't want a bridge. We want a tunnel," at the top of their squeaky voices. They were, of course, led by the Mesdames Mole, Weasel, Stoat, Viper and Polecat, who directly after the Prince had left the scene, furled their banners, dismantled their placards and made their way to the back door of the council offices where they were let into the building by Ms Snappy-Yappy and were served with drinks and sandwiches that had been put aside for them, on the orders of Sly-Fox. For it was Sly-Fox who had been responsible for orchestrating the demonstration, with the prospective foresight of cajoling his fellow town animals at some time in the near future, to enforce through public opinion and a petition, the completing of the tunnel under the M A / A track, that would lead into the Primary *High* School. By creating a public demonstration, he had planned to obtain a future lucrative contract from Animal Country Parkland Borough Council for RASCELS. After all, he wasn't known as Sly-Fox without good reason.

Ms Black-Widow Spider was tuned in through her own private website to everything that was taking place. She followed every move the Royal entourage made. While hidden in their hundreds of thousands in every nook and cranny, in trees and bushes, listening in on their own webs, her army of spinner spiders with their eight eyes, watched from vantage points along the Royal route leading to *their* spectacular footbridge creation, *their* technological engineering marvel for which not a single one of them, including their Managing Director, had received a word of thanks or a grateful acknowledgement for *their* footbridge creation that spanned the M A / A track junction.

When the Prince reached the footbridge site off Old Church Lane, there were thousands of flags being waived by the good-natured, loyal animals of Animal Country Parkland that had been waiting patiently for his arrival and who welcomed him with rapturous applause. It was then as the Prince alighted from the Royal carriage and stepped towards the footbridge entrance that the Mayoress, Mrs Gobbler Turkey, who had been hurriedly whisked away from the council offices to the footbridge site for the purpose, was already waiting to hand the Prince a pair of rolled gold plated scissors, with which he could cut the silk tape. It was to be an act that heralded the opening of the footbridge, so that His Royal Highness could proclaim it to be named, 'The Queen Beth Bridge'. After the Prince had named the bridge and cut the tape, Mrs Gobbler Turkey invited His Royal Highness to walk with her across the footbridge and as she had been instructed by Sly-Fox, she beckoned to a cat with a fiddle that had been conveniently standing close by, to start playing a tune. She then gestured to all the young animals to follow them and to the cheering of the crowd and the singing of the school's choir, the Royal Prince, Mrs Gobbler Turkey and hundreds of the pupils of the Primary *High* School, all singing at the top of their voices, skipped along behind Prince Porpoise just as the children in Robert Browning's famous poem 'The Pied Piper of Hamelin' had skipped behind the piper. It was an event that brought even more thunderous applause from the crowds.

The Prince was thoroughly bemused by the spectacle and entranced by the enthusiasm and loyalty with which the populous of Animal Country Parkland had welcomed him. It appeared to the Prince now that all the adverse publicity directed personally towards him by national and international media organisations in their continuous reporting of an 'extra-marital' relationship had never taken place. There was no doubting the Prince had enjoyed being among the loyal, ordinary animals of Animal Country Parkland and he showed some reluctance in having to leave them in order to attend a reception that had been organised supposedly for 'His' benefit but was actually designed to give all those toadies and hangers-on that had not been introduced to him prior to the opening of the footbridge, a chance to do a bit of grovelling and kowtowing to His Royal Highness on their own account.

The reception that followed the opening of the footbridge was held well away from Animal Country Parkland. This was due to advice given to the Prince by the Royal Protection Group based on the advice of

Sniffer Blood Hound the senior police hound, who himself had been ordered to do so by Sly-Fox for reasons best known only to Sly-Fox. The reception was therefore held in the grounds of 'Peacocks Gable Farm' behind high security fences, where Lord Cock-of-the Hoop Peacock and Lady Peahen Peacock, both of whom were close friends of the Prince, welcomed him.

The Prince, wearing white gloves over his fins, shook the paws, talons or claws of every toady that was presented to him by His Worship the Mayor. While his erstwhile host, Lord Cock-of-the Hoop Peacock, strutted about his domain with tail feathers spread out as beautifully as any Chinese multi-coloured silk fan. Occasionally, if the mood took him, he condescended to stop and talk to those animals he deemed to be worthy of his interest, whilst those he thought to be well below his status were shunned as though they were suffering from bubonic plague, the pox or in the case of poor timid rabbits, myxomatosis.

Sly-Fox, on the other hand, circulated easily among the 'well-to-do' assembled animals of Country Parkland, shaking their paws, talons or claws and kissing cheeks, so as to be seen as the 'fellow-well-met' type of fox. It was an upmarket *jack-the lad* image that he specifically set out to portray to his fellow partisan citizens; for he never missed a sly trick when it came to promoting his own interests. He had learned quite a bit about psychic-inducement from his wife, who had majored in both 'classical cunning' and 'perverted deviousness' in the University of Life. So he took the golden opportunity when he came upon Freddy (Croaky) Frog, Animal Country Parkland's society's renowned tittle-tattle to say,

"You know Croaky my old amphibious friend, I know you can keep a secret but I must tell someone. I'm beginning to feel awfully embarrassed. Several acquaintances of mine have suggested my name should be forwarded to the Cabinet Office for nomination of a Knighthood, based mainly on my work in getting the footbridge constructed over the M A / A track junction. They've even suggested Black Rat should be elevated to the Peerage for the support he gave *me* in the House of Common Animals."

"I'm not surprised at that, Foxy," croaked Freddy Frog. "The footbridge was a brilliant idea. It's so cleverly designed that one cannot see a weld or rivet join in it anywhere. It's cosmetically beautiful too. Reynard's and Serpents did an absolutely marvellous job getting the work completed in such a short time."

"Oh! They did, did they?" replied a bemused Sly-Fox. With a broad, mischievous grin on his face he then winked at Freddy Frog before saying, "Yes, but one had to chivvy those damn contractors along to get the best results out of them and one did just that, didn't one?"

"Yes, I'm sure one did," croaked Freddy Frog and continued, "but one cannot help thinking the design of the footbridge is rather an inverted web shape, can one?"

"Erm, yes! I do suppose to some extent one could say that, couldn't one?" and before Freddy Frog could ask any awkward questions, Sly-Fox said, "I'd better get on circulating. Nice seeing you again Croaky old friend." Then, as Sly-Fox trotted away from Freddy Frog he raised his bark and said, "A Knighthood for me, a Peerage for Black Rat, Croaky. The things one hears from one's friends and I wonder who would promote such an idea on our behalf. Ha, ha, ha?"

As Sly-Fox retreated from Freddy Frog's company, out of the corner of his eye Sly Fox watched as Freddy Frog hopped across the lawn and began talking to Lord Cock-of-the-Hoop Peacock, who raised his head, fanned out his tail feathers to their fullest extent then turned and glanced in Sly-Fox's direction. Sly-Fox began to chuckle to himself for he knew the seed of his deceit was sown.

Meanwhile, Prince Porpoise had finally finished his boring chore of paw, claw and talon shaking and after a short discussion with 'mine host', who Sly-Fox had noted out of the corner of his cunning eye, nodded several times in his direction before going over to where the Prince of Whales sea horse-drawn, swordfish escorted Landau was waiting ready to speed him off to his next official appointment.

Of course, what was not known to the Prince Of Whales, Lord Cock-of-the-Hoop Peacock nor any other animal not privy to Bridge Club Committee information, was that Sly-Fox's co-conspirators had already sent for, received and were ready to return a Cabinet Office Nominee form citing social and environmental activities for the benefit of all the animals of Country Parkland that Sly-Fox was said to have been responsible for promoting. All they required now was the full support of the Lord Lieutenant of the County - and Sly Fox was home and dry for a Knighthood. In the meantime, the same team of co-conspirators had approached the Prime Minister, suggesting Black Rat should be awarded a Peerage and elevated to the House of Animal Lords. There was an unsubstantiated rumour circulating in Animal Country Parkland that a large donation to party funds had been mentioned for this favour.

The ploy to have Black Rat elevated to the Upper House was to make way for Sly-Fox's nomination to stand as the member in the House of Common Animals for the borough of Animal Country Parkland and, to get Black Rat out of the way when it was discovered he'd been fiddling his parliamentary expenses by claiming, among other things, for the lease of a flat in the sewers under the House of Animal Lords – and what subsequently also came to light, was a claim for the mortgage payments on a flat for his mistress on a floating duck house anchored on a pond in the grounds of the ruins of an ancient Norman castle.

In the meantime, Ms Black-Widow Spider, having lost all tele-web communications with the 19th Green clubhouse and Bridge Club Committee room, immediately ordered a complete overhaul of her central tele-website system that covered the whole area of the golf links and golf club but with specific emphasis being given to the Bridge Club Committee's boardroom. She knew this was at the centre of all the underhand intrigue carried out in Animal Country Parkland and where the extermination of her cousins had been perpetrated.

Ms Black-Widow Spider's senior tele-web site engineer had therefore quickly designed single thread tele-web lines and had installed a large number of them that ran from either side of the Bridge Club Committee's boardroom to link up with pond spider's websites, sites that were suspended between reeds in the centres of their ponds and spinet spiders whose websites hung suspended in bushes and trees that surrounded the perimeter of the whole of the golf links.

All spiders on websites in Animal Country Parkland were under orders to be extra vigilant and observant as to the activities of Sly-Fox and his fellow councillor members, especially those members who sat on the Planning and Construction Committee, with special emphasis for them to keep their eyes on members of the 19th Green Bridge Club Committee. Also, Ms Black-Widow Spider wanted to be specifically informed about every movement that was made by the American, Fetid Skunk and the Canadian, Vic the Mink - and as she told her intimate friend, Tarantula-Spider after he had been reinstated in his job as senior security officer for Spiders International Limited, following the Royal Protection Group's withdrawal once Prince Porpoise's visit to Animal Country Parkland was over and they had vacated the area,

"Do you remember the nursery rhyme 'Little Red Riding Hood' where the wolf got into the grandmother's bed and Goldilocks said, "What big ears you've got, grandma?" Well, Sly-Fox is about to find out what big ears I've got! He's up to something that's devious, cunning and treacherous, which is his nature. When I learn just what that is I intend to deal with him once and for all. I'll teach that bounder a lesson in ethics and animal cunning he'll never live long enough to comprehend. You'll see."

But Sly-Fox was jubilant at the success of the Royal Visit. He immediately called an emergency meeting of the Bridge Club Committee for them to discuss his idea and the possible financial implications and ramifications of a non-residence 'toll' on the footbridge and the 'knock-on-benefits' that would be derived from such a scheme.

However, Sly-Fox had to admit there would also be an immediate 'financial kick-back', which could be derived from such a venture for RASCELS because the sheer pressure of use on the footbridge would help to induce, (with a little brainwashing from Mrs Sly-Fox on Mrs Mole), to inveigle her intimate friends the Mesdames Stoat, Polecat and Weasel to re-assert their demand for the completion of the tunnel under the animal track. It would then be through public demand that RASCELS would reap further rewards of a lucrative contract for the completion of the tunnel, which would have to include an additional clause in any contract for extra money to be made available in securing and sealing off the toxic impregnated sub-soil or for its removal and disposal off site.

After Sly-Fox had finished speaking, the dialogue that emanated between the other Bridge Club Committee members was based on what would be the best method of advancing the 'toll' idea to those councillors that were outside the Bridge Club Committee's immediate sphere of political influence.

"However," Sly-Fox told them, "that's not a problem. We all know how gullible and naive they are. I'll slip the idea in during the normal course of planning and construction business. Just a mention of reducing the local council tax will get the other councillors falling over themselves to vote for a 'bridge toll', you'll see." Then, in his normal way, Sly-Fox called the meeting to a close, got up and trotted briskly out of the council chamber without so much as a *'goodnight' bark* to any of them.

When the scheme to introduce a 'toll' on the footbridge for non-residents was slipped into normal council planning and construction business by Sly-Fox, supported by a recommendation from the council's

Senior Executive Officer, 'Slippery' Grass Snake, who contemplated getting a substantial bonus from any extra revenue a 'bridge toll' would generate for the borough council, the motion was voted to be put before a full meeting of the borough council as a proposal that if voted on and carried, may reduce local council tax levels by several percentage points for each household living within the borough boundaries.

The Bridge Club Committee agreed a proposal for a 'toll' to be levied on non-residents using the bridge. The proposal had been put forward by Councillor Sly-Fox and seconded by Councillor Dipper Magpie, JP. Dipper Magpie then arranged an interview with Nosey Parrot, a reporter working for 'The News of the Weald', in which he stated it was by sheer chance he, together with Sly Fox, had obtained a licence from Parklands Borough Council to set up a photographic emporium at each end of the footbridge. It had, by the terms of the licence, the power for franchised photographers to take portraits and photographs on the footbridge. The licence also allowed the promotion of sightseeing tours over the bridge and round the town. The proposal was carried unanimously.

PART 10

"Remind me, why did Sly-Fox arrange for that murder?"

Ms Black-Widow Spider was sitting in her office with her eight eyes half closed and with one set of her four legs crossed over her other four legs. She was deep in her own thoughts, weighing up the pros and cons in respect of the antics of Sly-Fox, his associates and his henchmen of the 19th Green Bridge Club Committee. She wasn't too bothered about what those scoundrels did in the manipulation of borough council policies to enhance their own line of business interests, either locally, nationally or even internationally. There were very few companies in the world that operated within the Laws of the Land in which they professed to serve, honestly and legally.

In many companies, national and international, company Chairmen readily admitted to enhancing sales of their companies' goods and services with 'golden handshakes' or 'backhand payments' both to corrupt and to corruptible officials. Such graft obviously happened more so in those countries where corruption is endemic from Presidents and Prime Ministers down to the lowest level of office workers, police and customs officials. Even

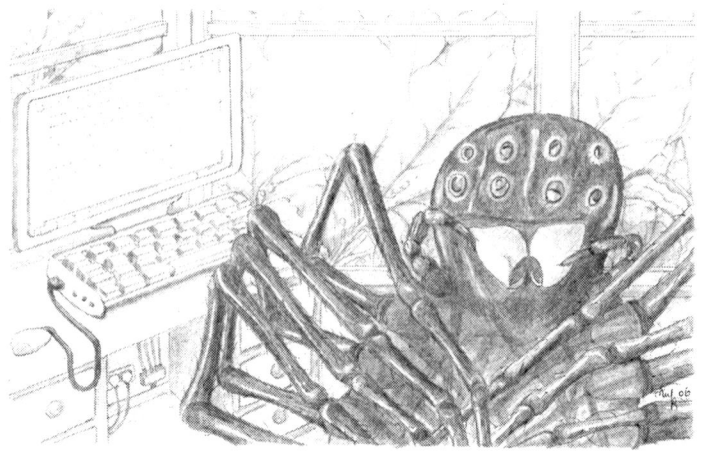

in such countries that boasted no corruption was permitted within their boundaries, political donations by rich individuals seeking titles or other honours and international companies were accepted as being the norm. But Sly-Fox, she mused, had gone beyond the acceptable level of devious corruption. The latest news coming to her over the website was showing just what a capable and manipulating scoundrel Sly-Fox really was. It was time for a recap on his criminal antics. Ms Black-Widow picked up the web-intercom and told her secretary, Ms Funnel-Web Spider, to drop any other work she was doing and come into her office and to bring her shorthand notebook and Sly-Fox's personnel records with her. As soon as Funnel-Web Spider had entered her office and sat down, Ms Black-Widow Spider told her,

"Now, I want you to make a full list of all the misdemeanours, criminal acts, murders or otherwise, that have been carried out against Spiders International Limited, on or against any of our cousins since our meeting with members of the Animal Country Parkland Borough Council's Planning and Construction Committee and the Directors of RASCELS Limited."

"Yes, Ms," replied Funnel-Web Spider, "but surely there were only two major infringements, weren't there?"

"Two!" exclaimed Ms Black-Widow Spider.

"Yes, Ms. The destruction of the 19th Green golf club and Bridge Club Committee's websites together with the murders of our cousins on those premises." Then she added, "Unless you intend to include the way Sly-Fox manipulated the death of Wiggly Worm. That was a classical, un-provable murder. He did it by insisting Digger Mole should employ Wiggly Worm to dig a pilot tunnel under the animal track, knowing full well the sub-soil was contaminated with arsenic and heavy metal. He knew worms cannot turn round once they start tunnelling, so when Wiggly Worm began to ingest the poisons in the soil, he had no option but to carry on. He simply just dug his way to his own death."

"Remind me, why did Sly-Fox arrange that particular murder?"

"Because Wiggly Worm was heard to make remarks saying, "There are no earthworm mounds on the old gasworks site; no earth mounds, no worms. There's got to be something wrong with the soil if there are no worms in residence." That has to be why Sly-Fox arranged for Wiggly Worm's death, Ms."

"Yes, you're right about that, I'd forgotten. But as far as we are concerned there are only two crimes that we currently know of, outsiders such as Wiggly Worm are no business of ours. I almost let my personal bias take over from evaluating the simple facts. I suppose that's because those recent snippets of information that came to me over the new websites have made the hairs on my appendages stand on end."

"Oh! What information is that?" said Funnel-Web Spider.

"Well," replied Ms Black-Widow Spider, "Sly-Fox is angling to get himself a Knighthood. That's all been laid on with the aid of his villainous friends. It's as good as been signed, sealed and delivered, once the Lord Lieutenant of the County, Lord Cock-of-the-Hoop Peacock, has made his recommendation to the Cabinet Office on Sly-Fox's behalf. The other two signatories to the recommendation are Black Rat, MAP and Councillor Venomous Viper, JP. Then, although Black Rat hasn't been told, Sly-Fox and his Bridge Club Committee associates have made a formal approach to the Prime Minister, Ms Nagging-Niggle, to arrange for Black Rat our MAP to be elevated to the House of Animal Lords.

"Why should they want to do that?" said Funnel-Web Spider.

"The idea behind this move is to make way for Sly-Fox's nomination and selection as the prospective parliamentary candidate for Animal Country Parkland. The conspirators' know Black Rat is under suspicion for over claiming on his expenses in the House of Common Animals. He's been claiming for a flat in the House of Lords sewers that his wife lives in and for a second mortgage on a house in the country, plus other numerous incidentals that include a duck-raft in the moat of his ancestral castle. When that information comes to light in the media, Black Rat is sure to be de-selected by his local party's nomination and selection committee. But if they can get Black Rat elevated into the House of Lords with some of the other crooks and ex-jailbirds that sit there, he will at least be safely out of Sly-Fox's way when the General Election takes place."

"So what are those scoundrels waiting for now?"

"I think it's for the publication of the New Year's Honours list. I know from my website that 'The News of the Weald' is already set to churn out thousands of copies congratulating Sly-Fox and Black Rat on what it describes as 'their well earned rewards for public service'. The information coming in over my private website is that they then intend to have a celebratory Gala Ball at the 19th Green clubhouse. I've got a list here of all those animals that are to be invited. It's the usual crowd of greedy, socio-economic parasites of the borough, their 'hangers-on' plus a few socially 'up-market' grandee outsiders, (old money animals), who unbeknown to them, are considered to be of some future use to Sly-Fox in his pursuit of high office in the government, when or if it is re-elected at the General Election," said Ms Black-Widow Spider.

"What high office is Sly-Fox after if he gets elected to the House of Common Animals?" Ms Funnel-Web Spider asked.

"Not if but when he gets elected you must mean. It's all been laid on, hasn't it? My bridge, after the deliberate failure of his tunnel project, so that he could dispose of Wiggly Worm, has been the key to Sly-Fox's plan from the very beginning of this charade. He's claimed all the credit for the bridge, from the planning stage to its construction, the cheat. He even had the audacity, the impudent devil, to claim that my bridge plans may become a major export product, though we don't know how he arrived at that idea because we lost contact when the websites were destroyed beneath the Bridge Club Committee's boardroom at the 19th Green clubhouse.

However, what we do now know is that scoundrel has pushed for and got borough councillor's authority to set a 'toll' on my bridge for non-residents of Animal Country Parkland. The latest news coming in over my website is that Sly-Fox has obtained backing from his councillor colleagues to privatise the bridge crossing and install 'toll booths' at both ends of its approach. But guess who is to get the franchise for what will be nothing more than a money-spinning racket? I'd better tell you because you'd never guess. It's Copenhagen House Toll Company Limited," Ms Black-Widow Spider said, her voice beginning to stammer in agitation.

"Really!" said Funnel-Web Spider, "but that is a subsidiary company of RASCELS and is based in Denmark isn't it?"

"Yes it is and Sly-Fox has manipulated the full financial benefits that shall accrue away from the Animal Country Parkland Borough Council to a foreign based company in another country. Of course, this has all been done with the connivance of the Ms. Nagging Niggle. Bitch government for reasons that we are not privy to. But a 'toll' on my bridge is as far as I'm going to let him go. We shall deal with Sly-Fox and those two assassins who killed our cousins on the night he is celebrating his greatest achievement, at the Animal Country Parkland Gala Ball. According to my information, the Gala Ball is being held at the 19th Green clubhouse on the evening of the 1st January. That's the day the New Year's Honours list is published and Sly-Fox's Knighthood shall be confirmed. I just can't wait to see his face when he comes into contact with my army of spinner spiders after the Gala Ball. I'll teach him a lesson he'll never forget – and it will be his last lesson too. His very last lesson!"

PART 11

The Black-Widow
takes her revenge on Sly-Fox

Sly-Fox had ordered that all invitations to the New Year
Gala Ball should be sent out in late November. Ms Pussy
Cat, 'Slippery' Grass Snake's personal secretary, was
assigned the task. The invitations were sent only to those
animals who, in the eyes of the Animal Country Parkland
Borough Council's Amenities and Social Committee,
chaired by Councillor Sly-Fox, were considered by him to
be worthy, upstanding citizens but who were more
important to Sly-Fox and his cronies because they were
influential and in most cases, were wealthy or ambitious,
greedy, blood thirsty and corruptible. In other words,
those socially and economically well placed animals that
lived within the borough boundary of Animal Country
Parkland and who literally did live off the sweat, blood
and fat of the land.

Invited also, were a few influential grandees from
various localities outside the borough's boundary,
animals that in the eyes of the Amenities and Social
Committee, in other words Sly-Fox and his associates,
were considered to be of some future use to them as
'front men' in devious business dealings for underhand

criminal business activities or just simply for *name dropping purposes.*

Also invited were several elected members of the House of Common Animals. They were chosen because it was known through Black Rat they were colleagues that could be easily corrupted if the price was right. Backbench members of the House who Sly-Fox knew he could rely on to assist him in pushing through legislation relevant to construction contracts, (contracts he intends shall be negotiated to the benefit of RASCELS), *when* he himself entered the House of Common Animals as the elected representative for Animal Country Parkland and, if all his devious, political pre-empting went according to plan, he would enter the government as its Minister for Trade and Overseas Development. When he thought about his future prospects as a Government Minister, he squint his beady, little eyes then rubbed his front paws together in gleeful anticipation at achieving that life-long ambition.

The invitation cards sent out were simple and to the point, they read,

<u>*THE MAYOR and MAYORESS*</u>
<u>On behalf of</u>
THE ANIMAL COUNTRY PARKLAND
BOROUGH COUNCIL
Have great pleasure in
<u>*INVITING YOURSELF, WIFE OR PARTNER*</u>
<u>To:</u>
THE BOROUGH COUNCIL'S GRAND BALL
That is to be held at

THE 19TH GREEN CLUBHOUSE
ANIMAL COUNTRY PARKLAND GOLF CLUB
On 1st January next from 8 pm
Black tie, carriages at midnight
Change to RSVP if not intentional

It goes without saying that the list of animals who were invited to the Grand Ball had, previous to the borough council's Amenities and Social Committee's meeting, been drawn up at the 19th Green clubhouse by the Bridge Club Committee. It was to that same meeting Black Rat, the Animal Country Parkland's elected representative to the House of Common Animals had, for the first time and for reasons he was told would later be made known to him, was also *invited* to attend.

Sly-Fox, once the committee was in session, pronounced to Black Rat that,

"The Bridge Club Committee is surprised but ecstatic, as no doubt you are about to be, at you having been proposed to be elevated to sit in the House of Animal Lords. Congratulations are in order but more than that, your life peerage that has yet to be confirmed has the Prime Minister's backing. It is seen by we of the Bridge Club Committee to be a great honour that reflects on the borough, also."

Black Rat sat dumbfounded. He sat gazing into space at the news that he was to be elevated to sit in the Upper House, especially as he had not been forewarned and the New Year's Honours list was not due to be announced till New Year's Day. He was shocked and bamboozled. He sat for several minutes like a zombie, seeming only to hear Sly-Fox barking out his professed congratulations from far away.

"You may be surprised to learn that your Bridge Club Committee colleagues have already discussed the matter and we're suggesting that you, the former Mr Black Rat, member of the House of Common Animals for Animal Country Parkland, should take the title of *Lord Black Rat* of *Animal Country Parkland*." Sly-Fox then raised his bark and said in what could not be mistaken for anything other than a direct order, "Such a locally contrived title will pull in a few hundred extra votes when you canvas for me at the forthcoming General Election. That is, of course, if I am selected to replace you by the constituency selection committee." The threat implicated in the tone of Sly-Fox's barks as he eyed each one of the Bridge Club Committee members in turn as he was making that statement was not lost on Black Rat. Neither were the glassy-eyed stares emulating from Fetis Skunk or Vic the Mink, the Bridge Club Committee's resident hit-animals, whose glassy-eyed stares implied retribution was at hand should Black Rat or any other member of the Bridge Club Committee fail to adhere to that intimidating command, as Sly-Fox began to be seized by a severe bout of power mania.

Black Rat, a normally rapacious animal whose ancestors had arrived in Animal Country Parkland from Asia many centuries before, (and brought bubonic plague with them that had wiped out most of the human population), sat rigidly upright on his chair, stunned by the news of his elevation to the peerage. He had not the slightest inclination or doubt that it was Sly-Fox and the Bridge Club Committee members that had orchestrated the move, which could only have been ordained by the personal intervention of the Prime Minister, Ms Nagging-Niggle, so as to pave the way for Sly-Fox's election to the House of Common Animals. It was a title that would force him to vacate his seat in the House of Common Animals but he was too wise in the ways and means by which Sly-Fox and his colleagues had obtained their information; too wise, that is, to ask any questions as to how the Bridge Club Committee came by such intelligence. However, it was certain a mole working undercover in the Cabinet Office must have leaked the information to them, as it had the information relating to an Order of Animal Country (OAC) to Councillor Venomous Viper, JP and the Member of Animal Country (MAC) to 'Slippery' Grass Snake, Senior Executive Officer at the Animal Country Parkland Borough Council.

It was soon after the '*advice*' given to Black Rat during the Bridge Club Committee's selection for him of his new title when, as was his way, Sly-Fox called the meeting to a hasty close with a few final barks of, "I'll see you all at the Grand Ball." He then dashed off out of the Bridge Club Committee room as quickly as his long, thin, furry legs would carry him.

Ms Black-Widow Spider had sat by her website together with her secretary Ms Funnel Web Spider listening in on the whole of the Bridge Club Committee's discussions. Then she said,

"It would appear that the greater self seeking scoundrels are, the greater are their financial rewards and the *higher* are the honours received by them from the State through the Cabinet Office. However, *higher* in Sly-Fox's case is not exactly what he thinks it means because I'm about to arrange a lesson for him on what higher really can mean. At this moment he's wrapped up in himself; full of pomp and self-importance that's verging on a severe bout of megalomania. Now, my dear Funnel-Web Spider, this is what I intend to do on the night of the Grand Ball." She then went on to outline her plans.

A full, watery moon was low in the heavens. Small white clouds were occasionally passing under the face of the moon, making it look as if the moon's surface was a slow cascade of yellow rippling water. A thick, heavy frost lay over the grass and covered the tall pine trees that surrounded the whole of the golf course. It was 9 pm on New Year's evening and the invited revellers at the Grand Ball were, as usual, having a glorious time at the local council rate payer's expense.

Gobbler Turkey and Mrs Gobbler Turkey, JP, wearing their gold chains of office as the current incumbents as Mayor and Mayoress of Animal Country Parkland, had stood by the door to welcome their guests. Lord Cock-of-the-Hoop Peacock with Lady Peahen Peacock were first to arrive. Lady Peahen Peacock was attired in her usual drab, brown feathered dress but he, My Lord Cock-of-the-Hoop Peacock, was in his official, flashy, feathered uniform and when the orchestra began to play, he went strutting about the dance floor with his tail feathers spread in all their glory just to let all and sundry at the Grand Ball know how important he was. After all, he was the Lord Lieutenant of the County, the Sovereign's personal representative for Animal Country Parkland, Cantium.

Councillor Sly-Fox and his wife, a vivacious vixen attired in her best winter fur coat was a real eye catcher as too was Ms Mink, wearing a pure white sable.

'Slippery' Grass Snake and Councillor Venomous Viper, JP, had shed their old skins and were attired in new, shiny skins; skins that glistened in the flashing lights generated by hundreds of female glow-worms (lampyris noctiluca) who had been hired for the evening to provide candescent lighting for the ballroom.

The orchestra, made up of a number of different animals under the direction of a cricket, with Ms Chirpy Chaffinch and Mr Sonant Song Thrush giving the vocal accompaniments, were a great success. Cricket, the orchestra leader, had done his homework, for among the most popular pieces played that evening were the Turkey Trot, the Fox Trot, Animal Crackers as a quick step and the Charleston. The penguin waiters, waitresses and barmen were rushed off their tiny flippers as they circulated among the toffs, nobs, snobs and well-to-do's of Animal Country Parkland - all of them totally oblivious as to the drama that was about to unfold - as the Black-Widow was about to take her revenge on Sly-Fox and his henchmen. It happened like this:

Fetid Skunk and Vic the Mink were told by the Master of Ceremonies, Mr Cock Bantam, Esq., that they were wanted outside to deal with some noisy Nightjars that were singing in the bushes at the rear of the 19th Green clubhouse. The two hoodlums left the clubhouse by the rear door so as to come up behind their intended victims in a surprise pincer movement but they only managed to get as far as where the bushes were beside the stream that led under the Bridge Club Committee's boardroom; that's where they were met not by passive Night Jars - nor Nightingales - but by an airborne army of spinner spiders that dropped down on them from bushes and trees growing beside the stream and also by water skater spiders that raced towards them from the surface of the stream running under the clubhouse.

Neither of them had a chance to call out and before either of them realised what was happening, they were trussed up in layer after layer of gossamer, like cotton wool gift-wrapped packages, then lifted onto the shoulders of the water spiders that skated over the water with them and took them to the very spot under the Bridge Club Committee's boardroom where they had exterminated all the resident spiders on Sly-Fox's orders. They were not killed; the Black-Widow had ordered they were not to be. They were hung up beneath the boardroom rafters, wrapped in fine gossamer like the Pharaohs of ancient Egypt had been wrapped in swaddling cloth and where their mummified bodies still hang to this very day. Silent witnesses to the carnage they caused that finally brought about their own slow demise.

On the other hand, Sly-Fox had enjoyed a wonderful

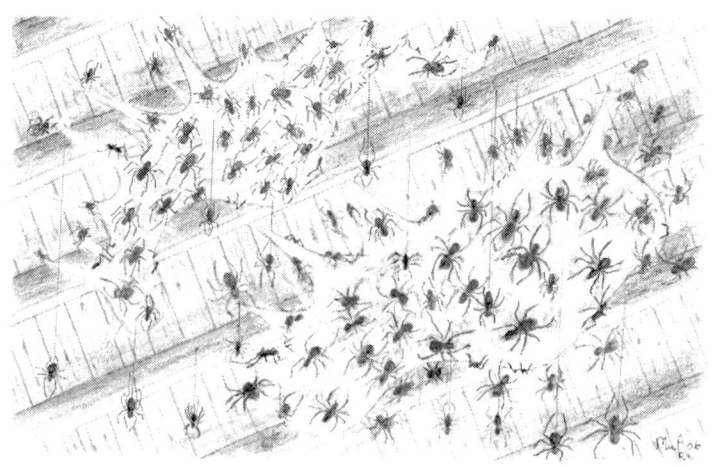

evening. He had had his hand shaken and been kissed so much that he thought he may have a dislocated wrist and a chapped face. He had so much lipstick on his cheeks he began to resemble a circus clown that was till Mrs Sly-Fox intervened to put an end to such shenanigans. After all, once Sly-Fox had received his Knighthood she would be Lady Sly-Fox and she had no intention of allowing any 'fly-by-night' sex-wacky tart or upwardly mobile bimbo, of which there were several at the Grand Ball, to relieve her of her future title and fortune. However, it wasn't the females at the Gala Ball that Mrs Sly-Fox had to worry about. It was a female from without whom she knew nothing about. To be more specific, it was Ms Black-Widow Spider.

At precisely 11.55 pm, Sly-Fox was informed by the Master of Ceremonies, Mr Cock Bantam, Esq., with the news,

"Your carriage awaits you outside the side door entrance of the clubhouse, Sir. I was asked to tell you by a penguin waiter that your lady wife is already in your carriage waiting for you and she apparently said, "You had better get a move on, or else."" Mrs Fox did not expound to the waiter what she meant by 'or else'. He then laughed and said, "But I wouldn't hang about if I were you, Sir."

Sly-Fox was surprised at this turn of events because he hadn't seen his mate leave the ballroom and there were only two keys to the side door entrance. He himself held one and Mr House Mouse, the golf club's resident steward, had held the only other key but Mr House Mouse had disappeared in mysterious circumstances and could not be found, nor could the second key. However, Sly-Fox having been well fortified from glasses filled with Ambrosia Nectar, gluttonous helpings from platters of good food and buoyed up by the music from a full orchestra (all paid for at the local rate payer's expense) and with his head beginning to spin as he launched himself out into the cold crisp night air, felt himself to be on top of the world. The door of a smart new chaise stood open and there were two pairs of daddy-long-leg spiders between the shafts waiting upon the order to convey the occupants to their destination. Without bothering to look inside the cabin, Sly-Fox raised one leg, stumbled on the low carriage step and fell head first into the chaise cabin, whereupon he was instantly seized and spun round like a top till he was bound so tight he couldn't move a muscle.

He lay on the floor of the chaise feeling sick from drink and dizzy from having been spun round and round like a top. As his senses returned, he realized he was being conveyed at speed and that there were other occupants in the chaise cabin with him. Then, for the first time a light came on and he saw that the other passengers were Ms Black-Widow Spider, the Managing Director, and Mr Tarantula-Spider, senior security officer, both of Spiders International Limited together with Mr Lasiodora Klug Spider, Ms Black-Widow Spider's chauffeur and personal bodyguard.

Sly-Fox looked about him and as he took in the scene he laughed,

"What sort of game are you spiders up to?" he asked.

"Game, Sly-Fox?" said The Black Widow. "We're playing no game. I am on my way to church to get married."

"Really!" said Sly-Fox, laughing out loud. "Who in their right mind on Golly's earth would marry you? To my knowledge, none of your 'would be' husbands have ever lived long enough to consummate a marriage." Then as an afterthought he said, "Have they?"

Ms Black-Widow Spider smiled. "No they haven't," she replied, "but never mind, your Best Spider is to be Tarantula-Spider."

As the Black-Widow finished her sentence the chaise suddenly stopped. She quickly got out of the carriage followed by Tarantula-Spider and making her way into the church, she stopped at the end of the aisle. The door of the chaise was left open and when Ms Black-Widow Spider and Tarantula-Spider entered the church, eighty daddy-long-leg spiders pulled the now quivering Sly-Fox from out of the chaise cabin and carrying him on their shoulders, they slowly walked him in through the church doorway and down the aisle towards the altar where Ms Black-Widow Spider was waiting for him. His Best Spider, Tarantula-Spider was by her side and behind her were two bridesmaids, Ms Funnel-Web Spider and Ms Red-Back Spider. The bridesmaids were both wearing long cream-white gossamer dresses, over which were draped capes of scarlet and gold dyed gossamer through which the cream colour of the dresses showed. They were, however, carrying wreaths of holly and myrtle in place of the usual bouquets or nosegays of flowers.

The church pews on either side of the aisle were filled with spinner spiders. There were spiders hanging by threads suspended from the old church roof rafters; there were spiders crawling about on the stone walls of the nave; and, after the daddy-long-leg spiders had deposited the bridegroom at the altar, more spiders followed them into the church to fill the aisle behind them. Every conceivable inch of the church was filled with spiders. They were even hanging from the bell ropes that dangled down from the belfry.

When Sly-Fox arrived at the end of the aisle, he was unceremoniously dumped on the floor beside Ms Black-Widow Spider. In front of them stood a feral cat wearing a cat collar in place of a clerical collar, for it was Feral Cat that was to officiate as the parson for the wedding ceremony. The choir, perched on the choir stall rails, consisted of the Choir Master, Mr Rook; two Wrens; two Great-Tits; three Nightjars; three Nightingales and a duck that was perched on a small stall, all of whom were smartly dressed in scarlet and black robes.

As soon as the congregation was settled the parson began,

"We have come together on this bitterly cold and frosty night to join together in the marriage our brother, Sly-Fox, and our sister Ms Black-Widow Spider. But because this wedding has been arranged under extenuating circumstances, no banns have been called. However, I am duty bound by the laws entrusted to me by the Ecclesiastic Church Commissioners under the Laws of this Land, to ask if there is any reason why these two animals, Sly-Fox and Ms Black-Widow Spider, should not be joined together in holy matrimony? If not, then forever hold your peace."

In the pulpit above the parson's head, Lasiodola Klug, the Brazilian Heavyweight spider, called out in a loud hissing noise,

"Cousins, I have reasons and objections why this marriage should not take place."

Then with two of his eight legs resting on the lectern rail in front of him, he began to read from a pre- prepared speech,

"I'm sorry," he began, "to call all of you, my kith and kin, out on what the parson has already described as a 'bitterly cold and frosty night' but it has fallen on me, first to act as the 'devil's advocate' by intervening in the proposed marriage of councillor Sly-Fox and Ms Black-Widow Spider and to act instead as a public prosecutor. This gathering is therefore no longer to be construed as being a marriage ceremony but a trial by jury. It is to be the public trial of Sly-Fox, specifically for those crimes he has committed against our well being as arachnids." Lasiodola Klug paused for a short rest as he painstakingly looked around the church to see what reaction he was stirring among his audience. He then continued,

"It is because of this change from a marriage ceremony to a criminal trial that I must ask the church choir to stand down and for those spiders among you who have volunteered to act as a jury, to take their places in the choir stalls. I therefore call forth the following volunteer spiders to act as a trial jury-

Ms Red Back, Mr Raft, Ms Orb, Mr Huntsman, Ms House, Mr Mexican Red Legged, Ms Moult, Mr Daddy-Long-Legs, Ms Scorpion, Mr Money and Ms Spinet Spider."

As the jurors made their separate ways to the jury box, Tarantula-Spider left Ms Black-Widow Spider's side in front of the altar rail and changed places with Lasiodola Klug in the pulpit. As soon as the jury were installed, Lasiodola Klug announced,

"Tarantula-Spider is to be the Trial Judge in the case of Spiders' versus Sly-Fox."

Sly-Fox shouted out as loudly as he could, "And who is going to represent me?" Titters of laughter came from the back of the church till the judge called out,

"Silence in court," he then said, "you have a good legal argument there, Sly-Fox. Your case is so serious that it warrants a defence lawyer but as no legally trained lawyer is available to undertake the task, you may use a Mackenzie friend to aid you in your defence, that's if you can find a friend. Now let's get on with the trial, it's getting late. Lasiodola Klug, if you would be so kind as to summarise the charges being laid against Sly-Fox."

"Ah! Thankee, Me-Lord, if it so pleases Your Lordship,' said Lasiodola Klug, emulating the phraseology used in the British High Courts of Justice. "If it should so please Your Lordship, I shall begin with the simple facts of this case. Those facts are contained in the affidavits of a number of the prosecution's key witnesses. For, as Your Lordship will be fully aware, Councillor Sly-Fox boasts he was the prime mover in promoting the idea for the building of a footbridge over the M A / A track that leads into the Primary *High* School. That was shortly after it was discovered the tunnel under construction by a Mr Digger

Mole, a specialist in subterranean tunnelling and a sub-contractor to RASCELS, was ordered to close it down due to the death of one, Wiggly Worm. Wiggly Worm had been employed by Mr Digger Mole to cut a pilot tunnel under the M A track but with the closure of the tunnel project, it was obvious another solution had to be found for a safe crossing of that dangerous track. At an interview with a Ms Nosey Parrot, a reporter with 'The News of the Weald', shortly after the inquest on Mr Wiggly Worm, Sly-Fox is recorded as having said,

"Damn that accident, now we shall have to build a footbridge and that means calling in the arachnids."

The building of a footbridge was said to have been for the benefit of getting young animals safely to and from the Primary *High* School and when Spiders International Limited was approached on the subject of constructing a footbridge, Ms Black-Widow Spider accepted a plea from the Animal Country Parkland Borough Council that a footbridge over the notoriously dangerous M A / A track was essential and so she gave the project priority status. However, it came to her notice via the website network that the objective of Sly-Fox's so called benevolence in first building an underpass then when that project failed for the construction of a bridge, was to advance the interests of an international civil engineering company, namely Reynard's, Serpents, Stoats and Weasels, Civil Engineering Company Limited. However, it was not unknown to Spiders International Limited that RASCELS is an international, commercially operating, criminal organisation, split up into various subsidiary companies to exploit civil engineering contracts worldwide. We know this simply because Spiders International Limited transmission and receiving website systems monitor all communications worldwide. But it has to be admitted I'm ashamed to say, we spiders underestimated the resolve of the 19th Green golf club's Bridge Club Committee's Chairman, Sly-Fox, when he began to use our spider facilities and power to the benefit of the RASCELS organisation to his own ends."

"Stop right there," ordered Tarantula-Spider. "I understood you were going to outline the facts not set about filibustering this case out of time. Dawn will be breaking before we get a verdict if you carry on gabbling. But before you go on, have you any questions you wish to ask the prosecutor, Sly-Fox?"

"Yes!" Sly-Fox began to bark out but was immediately interrupted by Tarantula-Spider who said,

"Stop your whingeing, Sly-Fox. I'm in charge of this court and if there is any pointing out to be done, I'll do it. You just lie where you are, stay silent and listen to the prosecutor. Right, Lasiodola Klug, carry on and keep it brief."

"Yes, Me-Lord. Ah! Where was I? Oh yes, be brief. Then I place before the court the affidavits signed by the following,

Mr Digger Mole on the death of Wiggly Worm; Mr Daddy-Long-Legs Spider, senior Communications and Service Engineer whose affidavit relates to the destruction of Spiders International Limited website equipment on, in and about the precincts of the 19th Green clubhouse. That affidavit also relates to the late Messrs Fetis Skunk and Vic the Mink's murder of our cousins in and under the Bridge Club Committee boardroom at the 19th Green clubhouse." Lasiodola Klug then stopped to take a sip of water before continuing,

"Finally, I have a copy of a petition signed by several hundred animals stating their objections to the 'toll' imposed on visitors who come to Animal Country Parkland to see the wonderful bridge created by the spinner spiders of Spiders International Limited."

"Where did you get that document, Lasiodola Klug? It is not a document of which I had any knowledge," said Tarantula-Spider.

"No, Me-Lord?" replied Lasiodola Klug. "It's a document that was passed to me by a *mole* working in the borough council offices. Sly-Fox and his cronies are not the only animals that have their inside informants."

"Obviously not," replied Tarantula-Spider. Then he said, "I have read the affidavits so in the absence of a court usher you will pass them on to the jury to peruse. As soon as they have read them they shall retire so as to be able to arrive at a verdict."

The affidavits were passed to the jury, each member of which quickly scanned them and returned them to Lasiodola Klug. It was then that Tarantula-Spider asked,

"Have you elected a foreman of the jury to give a verdict on each of the charges?"

"No, we haven't," said Huntsman Spider, "but I'll do the job myself if it will save some time, if that's all right with you, Me-Lord?"

"Yes, perfectly all right," said Tarantula-Spider, "the court is quite prepared to accept that situation provided your jury colleagues are." The other jurors nodded their heads in agreement and Tarantula-Spider continued,

"On the first charge of Sly-Fox being responsible for the death of Wiggly Worm, do you find the defendant guilty or not guilty?"

Without consulting any of the other jury members, Huntsman Spider simply said,

"We don't see as the death of this worm has anything to do with any of us, after all, worms is worms - they're not spiders. We'll leave that decision up to you if you don't mind Me-Lord?"

"Very well!" replied Tarantula-Spider, then added, "Yes, I do see the logic of your answer on that one but I had better call it guilty to be on the safe side. Is that OK with the jury?"

"Yes, that sounds about right to us," said Huntsman Spider, again without consulting his colleagues. "What's next?"

Sly-Fox managed to bark out, "This is nothing but a Kangaroo Court; I don't recognise its authority."

"Oh! You don't - don't you, Sly- Fox?" said Tarantula-Spider glaring down at him from the pulpit, "but you shouldn't worry yourself too much on that score because this court recognises you. It recognises you for the ambitious, vindictive, conniving, vicious, underhand, megalomaniac, rapscallion murderer you really are," then he continued by way of an aside that brought a murmur of low laughter from the spiders hanging in the rafters, "and those are just your better qualities; I won't try to name your good points because there's no evidence to show whether you have ever had any."

This comment produced a further bout of low laughter from the assembled spiders till Tarantula-Spider banged a mallet and ordered, "Silence in court." Then, turning to the jury he asked, "How do you find the defendant on the charge of the destruction of Spiders International Limited website equipment at the 19th Green clubhouse premises?"

"Guilty as charged," replied Huntsman Spider.

"And on the charge of incitement to murder and for being responsible for ordering the deaths of our cousins at the 19th Green clubhouse premises; how do you find the defendant on that count, guilty or not guilty?"

"We, the jury, find the defendant guilty on all the charges," said Huntsman Spider. Then turning his eight eyes to look in every direction of the church alter he said, "And all those other crimes he's perpetrated with his criminal cronies, crimes with which he's not been charged and crimes he would commit if he is allowed to go free from this court."

"Oh!" said Tarantula Spider, "I hadn't thought of the crimes to be taken into consideration (CTBTIC) but I'll take them into consideration now, just to clear up all those crimes outstanding on our records." He then sat in silence for a few moments with his eyes closed before he said,

"Right. Stand up, Sly-Fox."

Sly-Fox barked out, "How can I? I'm bound paw to paw."

"Well," replied Tarantula-Spider, "in that case you'd better lie where you are. As you have heard, Sly-Fox, the jury has found you guilty on all those charges brought against you. What's more, I've allowed them to include those other crimes listed at Spiders International Security Services Limited as crimes to be taken into consideration. That, by the way, is so we can clear out your criminal personnel record. I'm sure you won't mind?"

"Mind? What difference does it make?" rasped Sly-Fox, "I don't recognise your authority to charge me with anything."

"You don't, Sly-Fox! Nor does anyone in this court expect you to. Murderers of innocent animals, political assassins, contract murderers, religious fanatics and others of their ilk the world over, whatsoever their motive, or simply because they are psychopathic, homicidal maniacs that kill for the enjoyment of seeing other animals suffer, they all say the same thing, "We don't recognise the authority of this court." Well, there's one thing you can be sure of, Sly-Fox, this court recognises you and your crimes," and with no more ado Tarantula-Spider took a black cap from off the top rail of the pulpit, pulled it firmly down over the top of his head and said,

"Sly-Fox, for all those crimes you have perpetrated against our cousins and more especially, those of the murders you instigated and ordered of our kith and kin at the 19th Green clubhouse, I hereby sentence you to death. You shall now be taken to a place of your execution where you shall be hanged by whatever means your accusers should choose, till you are dead. May the great Lord Golly have mercy on your soul, if you ever had one. Take him down."

The daddy-long-legs spiders that had brought Sly-Fox into the church came forward and picked him up. They carried him out of the church followed by a multitude of spinet spiders, all of whom had re-charged their spinnerets especially for the job now to be carried out. They made their way jubilantly but in silent procession to the 19th Green clubhouse, (the scene of the boardroom massacres), and quickly swarming up onto its roof, they began to weave a gigantic web from the spinnerets in their abdomens. First they made the framework of the web and then the radii, after which they wove the spiral thread in between the radii to form what can only be described as a large net. That was when Ms Black-Widow Spider took charge. She had Sly-Fox hoisted up into the centre of the web from where he could be seen in the light of the silvery moon from many kilometres away. She then ordered the Australian Red-back spiders to "Sting him into semi-unconsciousness."

Somehow it was impossible to believe that spinner spiders could have built such a web above the 19th Green clubhouse, a web that appeared to be attached only to thin air. What is even more difficult to believe is that it looked from a distance as though it was spun in the very centre of the moon and that the dark shape on the moon's surface was no longer that of a man but that of a fox. When all the spinet spiders had abseiled themselves down from the web, Ms Black-Widow Spider scurried up onto the web to be beside Sly-Fox. She then began to sing to him,

"You should have known you crafty knave; we spiders cannot be made slaves.

You should remember the nursery rhyme, advice that's stood the test of time.

That if you wished to live and thrive, you must let spiders run alive.

So, au revoir, bye-bye, chin-chin, farewell; for your crimes I'm sending you off to...

Well! You know where I mean, Sly-Fox. I'll see you at *breakfast time* later on this morning."

Ms Black-Widow Spider then scuttled off down the web leaving Sly-Fox transfixed in its centre. He was silhouetted through the waning light of a winter silvery moon, where in his semi-conscious state he was supposed to contemplate what awaited him in the very near future as he regretted his past sins. But, as the old saying goes, 'the devil looks after his own' and in Sly-Fox's case he most certainly did.

PART 12

Sly-Fox exits Animal
Country Parkland; Forever

As the fading light of the moon began to dip slowly below the horizon and the new day's sun began to rise to brighten the sky, a cockerel crowed, awakened by the dawn breaking and as others of its ilk followed, their clarion calls reverberated throughout the countryside, awakening Councillor Dipper Magpie, JP, from an uneasy sleep. The previous night's reveries and his over indulgence in the abundance of Ambrosia Nectar at the New Years Eve Gala Ball brought him back to life with a nasty taste in his beak, a diabolical headache and bleary eyes. He sat on his roost shaking his head as he tried to focus his eyes. He had been brought up strictly with the knowledge 'it's the early bird that catches the worm' so he continued shaking his head and stared up at the moon in an attempt to bring his eyes back into focus. He shook his head again in disbelief. Was he seeing things or was that Sly-Fox resting on the moon's surface just above the clubhouse? He shook his head again, flapped his wings then launched himself into the sky on a zigzag route as he made his way precariously over to the golf club to investigate this unique phenomenon.

At the same time as Dipper Magpie was shaking his head, slapping his beak and blinking his weary eyes, Willy Weasel was stumbling his way home across the golf course, awakened from a drunken stupor by 'those damn noisy cockerels'. He looked up as he heard Dipper Magpie fly over and he too thought he was seeing things. For there was Sly-Fox struggling to extricate himself from a giant sized spider's web. As Willy Weasel came up to the clubhouse, Dipper Magpie, JP, flew down and landed beside him screeching,

"I've just flown over that web on the clubhouse roof. Sly-Fox is wrapped up in gossamer and lashed to its centre. What shall we do?"

"Do? By Golly!" Willy Weasel shouted, "fly to Digger Mole's workshop and borrow a pair of web cutters before the spiders come back. They've obviously got Sly-Fox lined up for breakfast. You had also better ask Mole to let you have a pair of shepherd's wool shears. We'll need them to cut that gossamer shroud off that they've wrapped him in."

While Dipper Magpie took off heading for Digger Mole's workshop, Willy Weasel made for the 19th Green clubhouse. Dipper Magpie was soon back carrying a web cutter and wool shears in his talons, which he dropped onto the clubhouse roof. He then flew down to lift Willy Weasel, who was trying desperately to find a way of getting up on the clubhouse, up onto the roof. Willy Weasel immediately picked up the web cutters and snipped away at the web. As the strands were cut, Sly-Fox tumbled down from the centre of the web and landed with a thud on the golf club roof. Dipper Magpie quickly cut through the gossamer shroud with the wool shears he had brought from Digger Mole's workshop but

Sly-Fox just lay at his feet, shaking like a leaf and whimpering. He was in a fearful state; unable to move due to the venom he had received from the Red-Back spider's bites. However, Digger Mole, who had been made aware of the situation by Dipper Magpie, had alerted Dr Barn Owl who flew immediately to the scene with an anti-spider poison vaccine, which he administered to Sly-Fox through his rump. The shock of the hypodermic needle in his rear end caused Sly-Fox to jump high in the air, off the golf club roof, landing on all four paws in the soft soil of a flower garden, from where he got up and ran and ran and ran. He was never seen or heard of again in the county borough of Animal Country Parkland – and rumours went about that he had taken flight to America.

POSTSCRIPT

However, the legacy of corruption left behind by Sly-Fox had now become endemic. It was continued with alacrity by his cub, Foxy-Fox, Chairman of Reynard's and

Serpents Civil Engineering and Construction Company Limited, who was duly elected onto Animal Country Parkland Borough Council by those same politically naive, dunderheaded voters who had elected his father, Sly-Fox.

Foxy-Fox's election was based on a similar promise too; a manifesto drawn up and agreed to by members of the Bridge Club Committee. It stated:

'I shall endeavour with every sinew in my body to make Animal Country Parkland a safe and prosperous place for all its animals to live in.

I shall endeavour to procure the means to install a tunnel underpass into the Primary *High* School and to see that it is duly completed.

I shall fight with all my vigour against any increases in tuition fees for our university students.

I make this promise that our hospitals will continue to serve the public with the highest possible level of free treatment.

I shall fight to stave off any further increases in government and council taxation.

So help me by Golly.'

After the Bridge Club Committee had finalised Foxy-Fox's manifesto for the forthcoming election, they were asked by Foxy-Fox to raise their glasses and drink the health of his father, Sly-Fox, especially for his foresight in setting up the 2010 Bridge Club Committee, with all that it stood for. This was followed by bursts of barking and crowing as committee members sat wringing their paws, clenching their claws or talons, (except in the cases of 'Slippery' Grass Snake and Venomous Viper, JP, who could only manage the flickering of their forked tongues), in anticipation of the profits and power

Foxy-Fox's election would bring them; bark – bark; crow – crow; flick – flick; yap –yap.

The Bridge Club Committee's last act of deceit before election day was to inform the media of Foxy-Fox's manifesto and organisations that were owned and controlled by foreign owned publishing moguls, sympathetic and in tandem with the psychological and manipulative political practices that were to be perpetrated on the gullible electorate of Animal Country Parkland - in the name of **Freedom of Speech, Social Democracy, National Welfare and Social harmony.**

Lightning Source UK Ltd.
Milton Keynes UK
UKOW040038200912

199298UK00001B/5/P